A COLLECTIVE BIOGRAPHY OF TWELVE WORLD-CLASS LEADERS

A Study on Developing Exemplary Leaders

John R. Shoup

University Press of America,® Inc.
Lanham · Boulder · New York · Toronto · Oxford

Copyright © 2005 by
University Press of America,® Inc.
4501 Forbes Boulevard
Suite 200
Lanham, Maryland 20706
UPA Acquisitions Department (301) 459-3366

PO Box 317
Oxford
OX2 9RU, UK

Library of Congress Control Number: 2005921131
ISBN 0-7618-3159-2 (paperback : alk. ppr.)

Table of Contents

List of Tables

Preface

How do we cultivate the type of leaders society desperately needs and craves? This collective biography on twelve world-class leaders provides timeless principles on how parents, extended family, schools, universities, and civic, religious and military organizations can facilitate the development of exemplary leaders.

The biographies and autobiographies of great leaders reveal the importance of an involved parent, happy childhood, plethora of "apprenticeships," rich formal and informal education, a steady stream of prodigious patrons, gracious critics and a favorable fate in cultivating exemplary leaders. The emerging leader's progression through the seven influences suggests a leadership development model that nurtures the exemplary leaders that society desperately needs. Stage I involves parents, extended family and educators instilling a sense of purpose and calling. Stage II is the discovery of a context in which to focus the calling. Formal and informal apprenticeships and education enables the leader to find a niche in which to prosper and contribute. After the emerging leader moves into a formal leadership position, Stage III involves the emerged leader recruiting and retaining the right people who make the leader's labor successful. Permeating each stage are prodigious patrons who guide, encourage, support and goad the leader forward.

In addition to the biographical data, this study synthesized the various trends in leadership studies to develop a comprehensive model on leadership. A coherent theory on leadership has been elusive because scholars have focused on specific parts of leadership, without recognition of the whole. The biographical data and synthesis of various leadership theories demonstrates that leadership and leadership development are biographical with exemplary leaders sharing similar story lines in their development. While each emerging leader lives their story within the larger story of the social and cultural contexts, the seven identified influences and the three stages of leadership development outlined in the book illustrate the themes that will allow future exemplary leaders to emerge and finish well.

This book is intended to aid anyone interested in cultivating much-needed exemplary leaders. Sowing the identified influences broadly increases the probability of additional exemplary leaders emerging.

"Some are born great, some achieve greatness, and some have greatness thrust upon them" (Shakespeare, Twelfth Night, Act II, Scene IV).

"Where have all the leaders gone? . . . long time passing" (Bennis, 1976, p. 328).

"The only thing necessary for the triumph of evil is for good men to do nothing" (Attributed to Edmund Burke).

Acknowledgements

I am fortunate to have had many prodigious patrons throughout my life. My wife Margarita is a paragon of unconditional love, whose dedication has enriched my life in immeasurable ways. My daughter, Rebecca Joy, brings much joy to her mother and to me, enthusiastically living up to her namesake. My parents modeled much for me, so a study on how to make the world a better place is a logical extension of their support and encouragement. My in-laws, whose love and support has made life, all the more, a gift to be enjoyed. My teachers granted me new vistas in which to understand life. To God, who has blessed and guided my life, that I hope will prove useful for His purposes.

Quotes

From JACK: STRAIGHT FROM THE GUT by Jack Welch. Copyright © 2001 by John F. Welch, Jr. Foundation. By permission of Warner Books, Inc.

From MY AMERICAN JOURNEY by Colin Powell with Joseph E. Persico, copyright © 1995 by Colin L. Powell. Used by permission of Random House, Inc.

Introduction

Cultivating good leaders is critical to society. Without good leaders in even the most basic and smallest grouping in society - the family, devastating consequences for our society will result (Horn, 1997). Rightly so, the mission of every school and university, whether directly or indirectly stated, is to develop tomorrow's leaders in various cities, countries, occupations, careers, organizations, and institutions (Starratt, 1993). While leadership-training programs abound, the quest for developing leaders portrays an urgency in the task while betraying that leadership does not come frequently or naturally (Vicere, 1989; Bolt, 1989). Bennis (1976) believes "true leaders are an endangered species" and that there "exists an appalling mortality rate -- whether occupational or actuarial -- among leaders" (p. 328).

Undoubtedly, society will take as many good leaders as it can get. The high demand for quality leaders begs the question; where do the "good" or "exemplary" leaders come from and how do we get more? As society's primary socializing agent in the development of people; schools, colleges and universities seem especially poised for cultivating leaders (Cusick, 1992; Schien, 1989). Evaluating the life experiences of a cross-section of leaders from a longitudinal perspective is instructive for families, schools, churches, civic organizations, businesses, military, and government. Just as providing a tree with proper nutrients, care to the soil and pruning enhances its growth and fruitfulness, so it is with leadership development. Providing the right type of experiences and environmental conditions will facilitate more and better leaders emerging on society's landscape.

The leaders of this study were identified from scholars of the rank assistant professor, associate professor and professor in business management, political science and military science at tier-1 research institutions (Carnegie, 2001). The scholars were solicited via e-mail to nominate from their field of expertise six leaders in the 20th century who are, or have been, influential and widely recognized for their accomplishments. In addition, the scholars were asked to nominate from the six leaders they identified those leaders whose personal character and values make them truly exemplary.

The two most frequently mentioned exemplary leaders from each discipline that had two biographies or one biography and one autobiography were the exemplary leaders of this study. The two most frequently mentioned and less frequently nominated for exemplary leadership from each discipline that had two biographies or one biography and one autobiography were the competent leaders of this study.

The biographical and autobiographical sources provided a longitudinal perspective for this collective biography or prosopography. Implementing techniques from narrative research, hermeneutics and grounded theory, a pattern for the cultivation of leaders emerged as similar and dissimilar life experiences were revealed. The exemplary leaders for this study in politics were Mohandas Gandhi and Franklin Roosevelt; for military science George Marshall and Colin Powell; and for business Sam Walton and Jack Welch. The competent leaders of this study in politics were Mao Tsetung and Adolf Hitler; for military science Douglas MacArthur and George Patton; and for business Henry Ford and Bill Gates.

A stage model for developing exemplary leaders is presented. The stages reflect the sequence of major influences that played a determinative role in leaders becoming people of influence, accomplishments and exemplary stature.

A brief overview of the research on leadership is presented first to reveal the different characteristics of leadership and how previous models have narrowly concentrated on the parts at the expense of the whole. A synthesis of the various trends in leadership studies and the data from this research converge to suggest leadership is the sum of many parts and is truly biographical in nature with common themes defining leadership and leadership development. The book concludes with specific actions members of society can implement to facilitate the development of exemplary leaders.

Leadership Studies: An Overview

Trends in Leadership Studies

It is an understatement to say there has been much done in the name of research to understand leadership. "Leadership is a topic with universal appeal, and in the popular press and academic research literature there is much written about leadership" (Northouse, 1997, p. 10). Bass (1990) cites 7,500 bibliographic references in his *Handbook of Leadership.* Bass reports there are "as many definitions of leadership as there are persons who have attempted to define the concept" (p. 11).

While much has been written, much is still needed. Burns (1978) states that, "leadership is one of the most observed and least understood phenomena on earth" (p. 2). Rost (1991) believes the "Mt. Everest of leadership literature" (p. 90) has yet to provide a model that truly explains leadership. Part of the problem in leadership studies is coming to a universally accepted definition of leadership. Barna (1997) reports "unfortunately, there is no universally accepted definition of leadership" (p. 21). Ott (1989) reports, "the search for a comprehensive theory of leadership is a seemingly never-ending quest" (p. 251).

An inherent difficulty with leadership studies "is that neither the scholars nor the practitioners have been able to define leadership with precision, accuracy and conciseness so that people are able to label it correctly when they see it happening or when they engage in it" (Rost, 1991, p. 6). Rost is even more candid on the dilemma of defining leadership. Authors on leadership state there is no universal definition on leadership, and yet, "ninety-five percent of the scholars ignore the statement and write their book, chapter or article as if they know what leadership is" (p. 14). Rost also bemoans that most scholars on leadership perpetuate myths about leadership, as they seem to erroneously review leadership theories prior to explicating their particular view on leadership. "These summaries of leadership theory are ritualistically repeated by author after author, especially textbook writers . . . . A critical analysis of the leadership literature suggests that the oft-repeated formulas for categorizing leadership and theory are not accurate at all" (Rost, 1991, p. 18).

At the risk of ritualistically repeating the various leadership theories, there is merit in recognizing the evolution of the study on leadership as scholars strive for a coherent and universal theory. In addition, the inherent difficulties in studying leadership and its various definitions may well be a clue to the phenomenon of leadership. Leadership is such a complicated and value-laden enterprise that a single model may not be forthcoming. Just as there are many facets to a diamond, there are many interdependent facets to leadership that converge to determine the color, clarity, cut and carat of the leadership moment and process. In addition, like a diamond, the setting does much to reveal or hide a leader's beauty and imperfections.

The first and dominant framework in leadership studies known as trait theory or "Great Men" theory has left an understandably lasting imprint. As early as Plato's *Republic,* Aristotle's *Politics* and Plutarch's *Parallel Lives,* specific attributes and traits were considered the defining marks of a leader. Machiavelli's *The Prince* continued the tradition that the effective leader possessed specific character traits and abilities in the practical exercise of power. Galton (1869) in his study of eminent people contributes to the theory of great men by stating "no man can achieve a very high reputation without being gifted with very high abilities and few who possess these very high abilities can fail in achieving eminence" (p. 15). Carlyle (1910) sums up the assumptions of trait theory in his series of lectures on heroes, hero worship and the heroic history when he states, "the history of the world is the history of great men" (p. 13).

It is understandable that trait theory continues to emerge, as history is replete with men and women of great reputation who have accomplished great deeds that others have been unable to do. While a cluster of traits do differentiate leaders from non-leaders and are a necessary component for leaders to emerge, they are not sufficient in the making of a leader. In the early stages, it was assumed that nature or heredity made individuals great people and, hence, destined to be leaders.

The list of necessary traits kept expanding as additional studies identifying the essential traits of leaders, via close examination of great leaders, were completed. Stogdill (1948, 1974), Bass (1990) and Northouse (1997) synthesized the repeated themes or traits after surveying the breadth of traits from the plethora of studies. From a century of trait research, Northouse identifies a convergence of the surveys to five central traits of intelligence, self-confidence, determination, integrity and sociability.

A transitional point away from personal characteristics in leadership studies came in 1948 with Stogdill's review of 124 studies on leadership from 1904 to

1947. Recognizing some traits of leaders exceeded those of the average member of the group; Stogdill concluded "the qualities, characteristics, and skills required in a leader are determined to a large extent by the demands of the situation in which he [or she] is to function as a leader" (p. 63). While research on traits continued, a new direction on leadership studies focused on the styles of leadership.

The second stage of leadership theory is marked by parallel research at Ohio State University and the University of Michigan in the late 1940s and early 1950s that focused on task and relationship behavior of leaders. Leaders were revealed as having a high or low propensity of initiating toward structure and/or towards people resulting in different ramifications for the group or organization. While primarily descriptive of what leaders do, a culmination of the research from this period is reflected in the work of Blake and Mouton (1964). Blake and Mouton developed a managerial grid (with additional refinements, later editions were named the leadership grid) which revealed the various ways leaders fulfill the group's purpose. The horizontal axis represents low and high concern for results and the vertical axis represents low and high concern for people. The various quadrants represent specific styles of leadership exercised as a function of the leader's preference toward tasks or relationships. Accordingly, leaders exercised authority-compliance management, team management, country-club management, impoverished management, or middle of the road management.

With the recognition that leaders have different behaviors and styles, the next logical question was if certain styles of leadership were better for different contexts. This gave way to the third stage of leadership studies focusing on the specific context or situations of leadership. Hersey and Blanchard (1969), using a similar grid as Blake and Mouton (1964) demonstrated that the maturity of the followers in terms of competencies and commitments played a determinative role in what style of leadership was required in the respective quadrants. Depending on the maturity level of the followers, leaders directed, coached, supported, or delegated to subordinates.

Not as optimistic that leaders could adjust their style of leadership to the context, Fielder (1964) developed his contingency theory that states an effective leader must also match his or her situation. Variables such as task structure, leader-member relations and positions of power are the determinative variables as to what style of leadership will work best for the group or organization.

In the early 1970s, still sensitive to the context or situation, the research on leadership began focusing on the nature of the relationship between the leader and the followers, known as what Chemers (1997) refers to as the "second generation of contingency theories" (p. 44). The path-goal theory based on expectancy theory of motivation examined how leaders actually interacted with followers to achieve subordinate satisfaction and performance (House, 1971). The type of exchanges between the leader and subordinates were found to influence the employee roles, performance levels and satisfaction (Dansereau, Graen & Haga, 1975). The nature of exchanges between followers and leaders surfaced in a group of studies known as leaders exchange or linkage theories of leadership (Northouse, 1997; Chemers, 1997).

Another major transitional point in leadership studies came from the work of Burns (1978) on transformational leadership. Burns seminal work continues to influence the current research agenda in leadership. Bass (1985) and Bass and Avolio (1994) took the baton from Burns by quantifying and qualifying transactional and transformational leadership into what they believe is a cohesive, comprehensive, congruent and universal model of effective leadership. Idealized influence (formerly referred to as charisma), inspirational motivation, intellectual stimulation, and individualized consideration comprise transformational leadership. Contingent rewards and management by exception (active and passive) comprise transactional leadership. Aspects of trait theory, leader's behavior and style, situational variables, and leader-follower relationships appear to converge into one theory. However, the model is inadequate in its emphasis on idealized influence (many non-charismatic leaders practice exemplary leadership), it minimizes how the situation or culture enables, constrains or even substitutes for transformational leadership, and in explaining how transformational leaders develop.

An emerging trend in leadership theory in both the scholarly and popular press is a sage-like attempt to reconcile the complexities of leadership while appreciating the aesthetics of the phenomenon. Without a universally accepted definition on what makes for a good leader and the highly value-laden concept of good leadership, the literature is now replete with works that are more akin to the wisdom genre with spiritual overtones. Wren's (1995) *The Leader's Companion: Insights on Leadership Through the Ages* "draws from a wide range of sources: observations on leadership by classical writers, seminal articles from major leadership scholars, insights from recent observers which expand the frontiers of our understanding of leadership, and the wisdom of leaders" (p. xi). Boleman and Deal (1995), in *Leading with Soul: An Uncommon Journey of Spirit,* state on their jacket cover how the "heart of true leadership can only be found in the heart of the leader." By providing insight and wisdom in the spirit of ecumenical traditions, Boleman and Deal claim to address the essence of leadership. DePree's (1989) book, *Leadership is an Art,* is an oft-cited book illustrating the complexities and magical aspects of leadership.

Steven Sample (2002) shares insights and lessons from "twenty-seven years of experience as a senior leader at three major research universities" (p. 3) in his book, *A Contrarian's Guide to Leadership.* Sample repeatedly shares how some contrarian principles serve leaders better than conventional wisdom. Conventional wisdom does not work a good percentage of the time given the competing and complex dilemmas associated with leadership.

Without hard and fast rules to guide leaders, *Principle Centered Leadership* by management guru Stephen Covey (1991) is intended to guide the reader in how to resolve the many dilemmas associated with leadership. Popular writer on leadership, Maxwell (1998) combines antidotal data with various proverb-like sayings and principles in *The 21 Irrefutable Laws of Leadership: Follow Them and People Will Follow You.* Social researcher and pollster George Barna (1997) edited a book titled *Leaders on Leadership: Wisdom, Advice and Encouragement on the Art of Leading God's People.* The book provides wisdom, advice and encouragement from 15 contributing authors. Farson (1996) wrote a Business Week best seller with endorsements from leadership gurus and scholars, university presidents, and leading CEOs in *Management of the Absurd: Paradoxes in Leadership.* Farson provides Solomon-like perspectives illustrating how a contrarian view liberates and empowers a leader to avoid unintended consequences of certain actions and capitalize on the meta-rules of communication and organizational life.

Synthesis of the Trends

The trends in leadership studies reveal that there are many different aspects to leadership. While there may not be a universally accepted definition or model of leadership, as stated earlier, the inherent difficulties in studying leadership and its various definitions may well be a clue to the phenomenon of leadership. Like the three blind men who upon touching different parts of the elephant disagreed on what the object in question really was, even though they were all talking about the same elephant. The person touching the trunk reports it is a huge hose. The one touching the torso reports it is a solid wall. The person touching the tail reports it is a rope.

As long as scholars continue to debate each other over which facet of leadership captures the essence of leadership, without recognition that they are talking about different aspects of the same phenomenon, a coherent theory will be elusive. The debate whether leadership is trait, situational, relational, or sagaciously driven focuses the discussion on particular facets without appreciation and understanding of the other facets, or the whole "diamond" of the leadership phenomenon. Such narrow debates continue to obscure progress toward a cohesive model, do not answer what leadership is in its totality and provide limited insight on how leadership develops.

A coherent model may well be revealed when the different leadership theories, studies and definitions are synthesized. A model of leadership that integrates the different theories brings together the leader's traits and characteristics, maturity of the followers, organizational and group goals, and cultural context. A suggested model views leadership as an equilibrium between the person (the leader with a minimum set of traits) influencing (styles of leadership) people (followers and constituents) towards particular tasks (the group's goals) in a particular context (organizational and cultural settings).

Shoup and Reeder (2004) provide similar insight to leadership *in toto* in their analysis of 176 metaphors and their accompanying descriptions on leadership from scholars in various disciplines. They found support for the conceptualization of leadership as a triune concept, as the majority of the metaphors analyzed cohesively fit into one of three categories or meta-metaphors: Navigational, Pastoral-Parental and Performance.

The navigational metaphors emphasized the goal/vision and directional setting of leadership. The pastoral-parental metaphors emphasized the relational side of leadership, in which leaders serve, nurture and positively influence followers. The performance metaphors focused on the accomplishment of the task in a coordinated fashion with goals or people. The results parallel the synthesis of leadership theories suggested above, that leadership consists of interrelated facets; the leader (navigator), member-relations (pastoral-parental) and task (performance).

Leadership studies are complicated by the fact that there is a reciprocal and dynamic relationship between the group goals, the organizational and cultural context, the maturity of the people involved, and the caliber of the leader. It is at this juncture that the wisdom aspect of leadership studies adds to the theory. Making judgments and exercising wisdom may well occupy the center of leadership activity. Leaders and people make judgments as to what issues and concerns of the different facets of leadership need to be emphasized, at any one point in time, in relationship to the dynamic activity of meeting group needs and goals.

For a cohesive and universal model of leadership to be developed, a comprehensive view of the data is needed. New data and new methods that examine the development of leaders will provide a skeletal framework with which to see the whole by looking at the sum of the individual parts. Yet, one thing is certain, we want more exemplary leaders. The question of how we produce such leaders still remains.

Old Question: New Approach

Additional Research Warranted to Advance Leadership Studies

"Good" leadership is a subjective definition. People want and need good leaders and, accordingly, claim to recognize good leadership when it is present. Yet, if you put fifty people in a room to discuss good leadership, you would end up with fifty variations on what makes a leader good. People's perception of a good leader may be more a commentary on their personal idiosyncrasies than one that is a universally accepted definition. Just as beauty is in the eye of the beholder, good leadership is often defined according to one's beliefs, values and context. An extreme illustration of subjectivity biasing our definition of leadership is Adolf Hitler. Hitler was considered a good leader by the majority of German families living in Germany in the first half of the twentieth century, while considered evil by the rest of the world. Every leader seems to have his or her fans along with opponents making leadership a very value laden or moral enterprise and, therefore, difficult to define with precision.

Leadership is a function of what is considered important and ultimately right in terms of the end and the means to the end. It is in this vein that Hodgkinson (1991) boldly asserts leadership is, in essence, a moral enterprise. But, it is also more than moral. Being well intended and well informed is not enough to be a successful leader. Being right and doing what is morally right does not guarantee one will be a capable leader, in terms of having the requisite abilities to implement what is right, or gain the loyalty of followers. One may be a "morally good" father or mother, but be an inept mayor or principal, university president, teacher, or chief executive officer. Even more problematic is one may be a competent leader, but not be well intended nor well informed. The cutthroat business leader may be appreciated for his or her truthfulness in gaining the competitive edge, but not necessarily be admired for treating people as a means to an end. Burns (1978) saw Hitler as one who effectively wielded power, but not worthy of having the title of a leader.

A common denominator of all leaders, both "good" and "bad," involves an aspect of being "set apart" or what Chemers (1997) refers to as status. From being the primary spokesperson in a simple social dyad or triad, or to the head of the family, city, organization, union, profession, institution, state or country, there exist variables that set apart such people from the "non-leader." It may be personal influence or position and status in life. Rising to a position of status in a social context is typically evidence of leadership. The sanctification of our leaders is an extremely complex puzzle with multiple variables factoring into the formula for a leader, all the more for a virtuous or exemplary and competent leader.

It is assumed that most people grant leadership to those they perceive as virtuous and competent. According to Chemers (1997), Americans view their ideal leaders as people who "usually have an inspiring goal or an inspiring way of describing the goal; they are trustworthy, honest, and fair, and they are confident, optimistic, and energetic" (p. 19). Kouzes and Posner (1995) state, "good leadership is an understandable and an universal process" (p. xxiii). According to Kouzes and Posner, a good leader is one who most people admire and would willingly follow. Kouzes and Posner were able to operationally define an exemplary leader by consistent consensus on the practices of leaders from business, community, government, churches, and schools.

Initially asking several thousand business and government executives what they admire most in their superiors, Kouzes and Posner "identified more than 225 different values, traits and characteristics" (p. 20). Using content analysis and further evaluation, the list of admired attributes was grouped into 20 characteristics. Using the 20 characteristics, additional people were asked to select the seven qualities that they "most look for and admire in a leader, someone whose direction they would willingly follow" (p. 20). From surveying over 20,000 people from four continents and over 400 case studies, the overwhelming majority "admire and willingly follow leaders who are honest, forward-looking, inspiring and competent" (p. 20).

What is true for leaders is also true for organizations. Collins and Porras (1997) used a similar approach in their comprehensive research of exemplary organizations. They solicited from 700 CEO's, people in the know, nominations for the top five "companies he or she perceived as highly visionary" (p. 13). Taking the 20 most frequently cited companies and excluding those companies that started after 1950, 18 companies remained. Other successful companies in the same founding era with similar products and markets and few mentions by the CEO's were identified. These comparison companies were selected so the study could be expanded to include the question of what is essentially different about highly visionary companies as compared to others. In essence, the authors cite they wanted to "compare gold medal teams to silver and bronze medal teams whenever possible to give real meaning to our findings" (p. 15). Studying each company throughout its entire history allowed the authors to have a rich database from which to draw "timeless, fundamental principles and patterns that might apply across eras" (p. 17). Collins and Porras (1997) also demonstrated that discrimination between exemplary and highly capable performers could be accomplished.

Assuming most people admire and want competent people who do the right things as their leader, where do we get these exemplary leaders? Identifying the variables that contribute to the development of leaders with the requisite skills and knowledge base (competent) and who have ethical ends in mind and practice the ethical means to the end (exemplary) becomes critical in an age faulted for few such leaders. A fundamental mission of every school, college and university is to develop these exemplary leaders. Knowing what variables best contribute to the sanctification of leaders will equip those who are in leadership development.

Comparing exemplary leaders with competent leaders (people who are competent, but not necessarily the type people admire or would willingly follow) and evaluating the leaders throughout their entire history promises to reveal fundamental principles and patterns of development. Examination of the lives of the "best of the best" among two groups of leaders, exemplary and competent, from various contexts, variables influencing the development of leaders can be identified. These principles are generalizable to developing exemplary leaders and will equip families, schools, civic organizations, and government to sanctify even more virtuous and competent citizens than are currently being developed.

Borrowing from the seminal work on cognitive development by Piaget, moral development by Kolhberg, and personality development by Erikson (Specht & Craig, 1982) along with faith development (Fowler, 1981), this research suggests a similar model may exist for leaders. Just as everyone experiences various levels of cognitive, moral, faith and personality development, there appears to be a similar model for leadership. While Tucker (1981) reports that a "leaderless movement is naturally out of the question" (p. 87), the leaderless moment is similarly out of the question. It is reasonable to assume that every social interaction requires some level of leadership. Every youth and adult has had at least one leadership moment with some having more and some being better. By possessing a model with universal stages of leadership development, perhaps experiences could be generated at strategic points in people's lives in order to cultivate more leaders than are currently on the scene.

Bass (1990) sets a similar research agenda when he asks, "what experiences are necessary to make an effective leader?" (p. 911). While Bass (1985) acknowledges transformational leadership can be found in various walks of life, "the problem remains as to how to identify and encourage its appearance in the military, in business and industry, and in educational and governmental agencies" (p. xv).

Developing leaders is an urgent and noble calling for, parents, educators and members of society. Kuhnert and Lewis (1987) applied a constructive/developmental theory to transactional and transformational leadership. They believe an understanding of how leaders develop will be instrumental in the selection and development of leaders. Kuhnert and Lewis ask, "are the hypothesized stages of development invariant? That is, do all leaders advance through the developmental stages in the same manner, or do the patterns differ for different leaders?" (p. 655). Kuhnert and Lewis are very directive when they state "researchers need to identify the processes by which leaders develop from one stage to another" (p. 655). However, Kuhnert and Lewis' focus was on how transformational and transactional leaders construct their social worlds. Limiting their proposal to a constructivist/developmental theory, the emphasis of their model is on the characteristics of the leader that is in the tradition of trait theory. The interest of this research is to discover the external influences that shape leaders, in such a fashion, as to be set apart from their followers.

Burns (1978) believes biographical data "can be an indispensable tool in analyzing the shaping influences on leadership" (p. 53). Burns advocates an agenda for research stating that the analysis should include, not only the early years, but also the institutional contexts and reciprocal relationship between the leaders and followers. Burns goes on to state that students of leadership "cannot unravel the mysteries of the rise and fall of a great man unless we analyze not only the psychological and social influences operating in him in his early years, but the political forces that he both encounters and generates in his middle and later life" (p. 104).

Along the same line of thinking, Cruikshank (1999), a scholar in educational history, advocates the use of biographies as a useful approach to allow one "to be able to grasp the larger complexities that might otherwise elude us" (p. 231). Cruishank believes biographies enable the scholar to better understand the intricacies and nuances of a particular era, movement or culture.

Avolio and Bass (1987) and Gronn and Ribbins (1996) propose biographical research can contribute much to theorizing about leadership. Critiquing the limitations of present research on leadership as minimizing or ignoring the context of leadership, Gronn and Ribbins believe biographical research can provide a context and comparison for leadership development and identify attributes from various contexts. Gronn and Ribbins state:

> Nowhere, it seems, is there a satisfactory answer to Kets de Vries's (1993, p. 3) question, "What determines who will become a leader and who will not?" One possible antidote would be to devise a framework or template for ordering the biographical detail of leaders'

lives. This would permit the comparative analysis of individuals over
and against the systems or cultural traditions of leadership that
nurtured them. (p. 465)

Gaining a longitudinal perspective on many leaders allows for a meaningful
comparative analysis for principles of development. Gronn and Ribbins (1996)
discuss formation, accession, incumbency, and divestiture as four broad stages
in which to understand leadership development. Gronn and Ribbins assert that
biographical research can be a catalyst toward leadership reproduction by
identification of the significant variables that shaped the leader's rise to the top.

Principles of organizational development were obtained in Collins and
Porras' (1997) biographical study of successful organization. The authors report
that they did what had not been done before. They took:

A set of truly exceptional companies that have stood the test of time
. . . . and studied them from their very beginnings, through all phases
of their development to the present day; and . . . studied them in
comparison to another set of good companies that had the same shot
in life, but didn't attain quite the same stature. . . What makes truly
exceptional companies different from other companies? (p. xiii)

In a follow up biographical study of comparison companies, Collins (2001)
researched what principles make good companies become great. He and his
extensive research team identified a framework to help companies move from
good to great. In conjunction with his previous work with Porras (1997), *Built to
Last*, Collins sees *Good to Great* as the prequel. What Collins (2001) and
Collins and Porras (1997) did for organizations in terms of moving a good
organization to great and building it to last needs to be done for individuals.
What makes for good people to become exemplary leaders that will finish
strong? In a reoccurring theme, Collins (2001) reports that moving from good to
great requires finding "Level 5 Leaders" and the "right" people throughout the
organization. Society will benefit from research that identifies those variables
that influence the emergence of "Level 5 Leaders" and the "right" people.

As organizational studies have benefited from longitudinal and collective
biographical studies, the same methods can be successfully applied to
leadership. Burns (1978) believes a "cumulative and comparative analysis of a
large number of leaders should eventually provide stronger foundations for
generalizations and hypothesis" (p. 60). Burns sets an agenda for research when
he states, "what leads some to moral leadership and others to amoral or immoral
power-wielding? This is a frontier that scholarship must explore" (p. 59). Avilio
and Bass (1988) and Kuhnert and Lewis (1987) also see the need for future
research to incorporate longitudinal designs on transformational leadership.

Understanding the lifespan development of leaders can undoubtedly lead to
better training and development of leaders. The usefulness and feasibility of a

development model of leadership can be gleaned from Clinton's (1988) study of hundreds of historical, biblical and contemporary leaders. From his research, Clinton developed a six-stage development model of church leaders. Clinton sees leadership development as "a life of lessons" (p. 40) with which the development of maturing leaders can be directed. A limit to Clinton's focus on the inner-world of the individual leaders was advocating a trait theory of leadership and provided little guidance on how to influence people to want to become leaders.

The need for research to compare and contrast the lifespan development of a variety of leaders, using biographical and autobiographical data, comes from the recommendations of Burns (1978), Bass (1990), Avilio and Bass (1988), Kuhnert and Lewis (1987), and Gronn and Ribbins (1996). Leadership studies will benefit from a collective biography or prosopography on exemplary and competent leaders. We know what good leaders look like (traits), the type of activities (styles and behaviors) they engage in and what situations (contingency) may be best for specific types of leaders and the importance of the relationship of the leaders with other people. We know transformational leaders make a difference. We have insight and wisdom from the ages that will guide people into being better leaders. In addition to an integrated comprehensive model on leadership, we need to know more as to what causes the exemplary leaders to emerge.

An Additional Method of Inquiry for Leadership Studies

A prosopography on a group of leaders from various fields will allow timeless principles for developing leaders to emerge and provide a comprehensive context to understand the emergence and practice of leadership. The methodologies associated with qualitative research, specifically narrative analysis (Riessman, 1993), grounded theory (Strauss & Corbin, 1998 and Merriam, 1998), and hermeneutics (Hirsch, 1967, 1976; Valdes, 1987), lend themselves to the making of a prosopography on leaders from business, military and politics.

Stone (1987) advocates prosopography as a valuable research technique.

> Prosopography is the investigation of the common background characteristics of a group of actors in history by means of a collective study of their lives. The method employed is to establish a universe to be studied, and then to ask a set of uniform questions - about birth and death, marriage and family, social origins and inherited economic position, place of residence, education, amount and source of personal wealth, occupation, religion, experience of office and so on. The various types of information about the individuals in the universe are then juxtaposed and combined, and are examined for significant variables. (p. 45)

Biographical research is very common among leadership studies. Useem (1998) states, "one of the most effective ways of preparing for such challenges [leadership moments] is by looking at what others have done when their leadership is on the line" (p. 3). Useem evaluates the accounts of nine significant experiences of leadership moments that have affected history so that the reader can glean universal principles for their own leadership development. In order to discover principles of strategic leadership, Bennis and Nanus (1985) studied 60 private sector and 30 public sector leaders with outstanding reputations generated from business magazines and news reports.

Writing brief biographical accounts, Plutarch (circa 82 AD) compared 22 pairs of great Greek and Roman citizens in his *Parallel Lives*. His goal to encourage reciprocal respect among the Romans and the Greeks illustrates the didactic value biographies can provide. Smiles (1881), used biographies on a wide range of ordinary people as a source of instruction and inspiration for people, even nations, in his influential book, *Self-Help; With Illustrations of Character, Conduct and Perseverance*. Since its debut in 1859, *Self-Help* has gone through over 80 reprints. Smiles (1881) states, "biographies of great, but especially of good men, are nevertheless most instructive and useful, as helps, guides, and incentives to others" (p. 27).

Sir Francis Galton (1869) used, as a starting point, a biographical handbook published in 1865 to statistically demonstrate the role of hereditary in producing illustrious and eminent men. From the biographical data, Galton inferred eminent men (people of high reputation) in England to be 250 to every million. In addition, he inferred the prevalence of one illustrious person – "men whom the whole intelligent part of the nation mourns when they die; who have, or deserve to have, a public funeral; and who rank in future ages as historical characters" (p. 11) – to every million people. Galton demonstrated that "illustrious men have eminent kinfolk" (p. 6) and attributed the relationship to heredity without convincingly ruling out environmental influences.

For his statistical study, Cattell (1903) selected 1,000 eminent men from those listed in biographical dictionaries or encyclopedias and ranked them in order of those having the greatest average amount of space devoted to them. Cattell concluded it is "evident that there are two leading factors in producing a man and making him what he is – one, the endowment given at birth, the other, the environment into which he comes" (p. 359).

Using historical data of heredity, childhood and youth, Cox (1926) studied 301 of the most eminent men and woman of history who lived between 1450 AD and 1850 AD. The purpose of her study was to identify how genius youth differ from average youth. Her goal was to benefit posterity by allowing for early identification of geniuses so selection for appropriate education could take place.

According to Cox:

> The whole problem of the origin, selection, and education of the
> gifted is one of profound concern, now as in Plato's day; for upon an
> adequate solution of it depend the appropriate and sufficient training
> of children of ability, the conservation of talent, and a possible
> increase in the production of significant and creative work. The study
> of the heredity, native gifts, and kinds of education that have most
> contributed to advance those who in the past became the ablest
> citizens of our world has long been recognized as a means of
> throwing considerable light upon the conditions which may be
> expected to produce and foster genius in our time and hereafter. (p. 3)

Cox (1926) believed Galton (1869) demonstrated the origin of genius. Her
goal to identify the second element of promoting genius (early identification for
proper selection), which must, according to Cox, ". . . precede any attempt to
analyze the third element – the contribution of education" (p. 4). Like Galton
and Cattell (1903), Cox used the frequency of mention in bibliographical data as
the measure of eminence. She even used Cattell's list of 1000 men as her
starting point in selecting her sample of genius believing "in general that great
eminence is coincident with great genius" (p. 20).

In their book *Cradles of Eminence,* Goertzel and Goertzel (1962) used
biographies and autobiographies to assess the development of 400 people who
were of significant fame and good fortune to have at least two books written
about them and were carried in the Montclair New Jersey Public Library.
Goertzel and Goertzel provided a descriptive summary demonstrating that the
family's value system has the strongest impact on an able child rising to a place
of eminence. John-Steiner (1985) made a similar conclusion on the importance
of a stimulating home environment in her biographical study of 100 creative
individuals.

More entertaining, but just as serious, in developing universal principles for
effective leadership are recent books that examine the leadership lessons from
Ronald Reagan (Strock, 1998), Ulysses S. Grant (Kaltman, 1998), and Robert E.
Lee (Crocker, 1999). Roberts (1987) writes on the *Leadership Secrets of Attila
the Hun.* The book is endorsed by a variety of leadership gurus including H.
Ross Perot who is quoted on the front cover saying what a "great book . . . The
principles are timeless." Strock states that "leadership does matter and that it can
be developed in part from the study of outstanding leaders" (p. vii).

In his prosopography, West (1996) successfully uses "biographical,
longitudinal and reflexive methods and incorporates an interdisciplinary frame
of reference to chronicle, analyze and theorize the personal and sociocultural
dialectics of motivation in the biographies of adult learners" (p. ix). Cronin
(1995) reports that, "students of leadership can learn widely from reading
biographies about both the best and the worst leaders" (p. 31). Cronin goes on to

say that "while each biography describes how heroes go about the leadership business, there is a paucity of comparisons of different leaders with attention to similarities and differences of techniques of leadership" (p. 35).

Using biographical data, Burns' (1978) seminal work on leadership documented the lives of various world leaders and developed a model of transformational and transactional leadership. Burns states that ". . . biographical data, can be an indispensable tool in analyzing the shaping influences on leadership" (p. 53). While Burns applied development theories in describing the influences on various world leaders such as Gandhi, Hitler, Lenin, and Wilson, he "recognizes the absence of systematic explanatory theory" (p. 60). He goes on to state, "cumulative and comparative analysis of a large number of leaders should eventually provide stronger foundations for generalizations and hypotheses" (p. 60).

Collective biographies and autobiographies have proven useful in understanding leadership as demonstrated by Goertzel and Goertzel (1962) and Cox (1926) with people of eminence, Burns (1978) with political leaders, Bennis and Nanus (1985) with business leaders, Clinton (1988) with church leaders, and Collins and Porras (1997) and Collins (2001) with organizations. Biographical and autobiographical data on leaders provides a depth and breadth of access to the leader's life experience, milestones and shaping influences in their rise to a position of influence. Collecting similar themes from individual biographies into a collective biography will allow for the shaping influence of exemplary leaders to be identified and, hopefully, replicated. Moreover, additional data about how leaders rise to a position of influence will help in the formation of a cohesive, comprehensive and congruent theory on leadership.

Methodology

Similar to the strategy of Cox (1926), Bennis and Nanus (1985), Kouzes and Posner (1995), Collins (2001) and Collins and Porras (1997), a list of exemplary leaders and competent leaders were nominated by informed experts. Originally, university scholars in business administration, education administration, military science, political science, and religious studies from 100 randomly selected Doctorate-Granting Institutions, as listed in the 2001 Carnegie Classification of Institutions of Higher Education, were solicited. For reasons explained later, the business, political and military leaders nominated became the subjects of this study.

The scholars, for purpose of this research, were Professors, Associate Professors and Assistant Professors. The scholars were contacted via e-mail, obtained from their respective university's web page. Tier-1 research universities were selected with the knowledge that scholars housed at such universities tend to be engaged in active research and, therefore, as a group, are more aware of those who have widely influenced their area of expertise. One hundred out of the 151 universities were randomly selected in order to have an adequate yet manageable sample size.

Rather than the popular press or biographical indexes, scholars were solicited for nominees of influential leaders of the 20th century. It is a reasonable inference that scholars will have a broader and more informed knowledge base about influential leaders in their domain than the general public, especially scholars at research universities. The general public tends to get summaries and highlights of influential people after the story has been filtered through the mass media, which has its own agenda and a tendency to sensationalize in order to woo their audience. Scholars tend to be in a better position to have evaluated the context of their domain to know who the significant leaders are versus those who just may be popular. By training, scholars also tend to be more discerning and evaluating on their judgments in these areas. Generally speaking, tier-1 university scholars have a broader and deeper knowledge base that makes them much more informed, and they tend to be more discerning in judging who are the best leaders in their respective fields.

Professors, Associate Professors and Assistant Professors were solicited in order to get a broader base of nominations. Professors, Associate and Assistant Professors tend to be grouped by age and as result share similar values and judgments associated with their generation. By expanding the pool of scholars solicited, the number of nominees potentially expands, while at the same time the most frequently nominated may well cross generations in terms of being recognized for their influence and accomplishments.

The scholars were asked to nominate six leaders in their field from the 20th century who are, or have been, influential and widely recognized for their accomplishments. In addition, the respective scholars were asked to identify among their six nominations those leaders whose personal character and values make them truly exemplary. The word "exemplary" has a semantic range that will undoubtedly reflect the biases of the judges. By gathering consensus from the solicited responses, it is reasonable to infer that those identified at the top of the list will share similar qualitative characteristics that match the construct of exemplary leaders and competent leaders.

From the list generated from the survey data, the two most frequently cited individuals from each category and, relative to each category, who had at least two biographies or one biography and one autobiography to their credit, became the subjects of the study. Biographies and autobiographies provide an additional source of validation on who are considered influential and accomplished leaders in their respective professions. The biographies and autobiographies provide the data for evaluation of patterns, themes and variables in the development of those leaders who have risen to the top of their profession. The two groups of leaders provide opportunity for meaningful comparisons and contrasts.

The reason two sources of life narratives were selected comes from the sound Biblical principle in 1 Timothy 5:19 of not receiving an "accusation against an elder [leader] except on the basis of two or three witnesses" (New American Standard Bible, Lockman Foundation). Two chronicles on each leader provided a source of validation for the other. Quality life narratives would either validate or invalidate what the other was saying. Contradictions from the two chronicles were resolved by cross-checking a third source of data.

The criteria for selecting the biographies and autobiographies as the source material for this study added another aspect of quality control in the reliability of the data being studied. Whenever possible, a comprehensive autobiography was selected to gain first hand reflections on the leader's life. The additional selection criteria were based upon the publisher, author, nature of the endorsements, and comprehensiveness of the material. Scholarly publishers were selected over popular press whenever possible. Authors who had credibility as biographers and had access to relevant sources were given priority in the selection process. Also, biographies that covered more of the life span of the person being studied were given preference.

Since history is still waiting to pass final judgment on the contemporary leaders, choices for sources were limited to one or two narratives for Gates, Powell, Walton and Welch. Fortunately, with the exception of Gates, autobiographies were available on the other three contemporary leaders. The biographies for the contemporary leaders were found substantive and well balanced in their treatment of their protagonist. Lowe's (2001) *Welch: An American Icon*, Ortega's (1998) *In Sam We Trust: The Untold Story of Sam Walton and How Wal-Mart is Devouring America,* and Roth's (1993) *Sacred Honor: A Biography of Colin Powell* provided a critical and skeptical counterpart to the respective autobiographies.

Autobiographies on Gandhi and MacArthur were also used for this study. While autobiographies on Hitler and Ford were available, they were not used. *Mein Kampf* (My [Hitler's] Struggle) was filled with self-aggrandizing distortions and was written in 1924 (first published in 1939) prior to Hitler's rise to power as a national leader. Ford's (1922) autobiography *My Life and Work* was written while he still had another 25 years ahead of him. Ford's autobiography reads more like a how to business manual devoted to sharing his exploits in the automobile business. It was a platform for his treatise on education, money, charity, poverty, democracy, railroads, war, and explanations of his exploits without reference to family and friends.

Roosevelt, Hitler, Mao, and Gandhi had the largest selection of biographies available. The two biographies used for Roosevelt were intentionally selected from well-published and respected historians and biographers, James MacGregor Burns and Frank Freidel. Eminent historian Arthur Schlesinger, Jr. endorsed Freidel's biography on the jacket cover as "the best single-volume biography of our greatest twentieth-century president" (Freidel, 1990). The 844-page biography on Hitler was selected for its thorough details and the credibility of the writer as one of Germany's leading journalists (Fest, 1992). Payne's (1973) 623-page biography on Hitler was his sixth historical work and published by Praeger.

Terrill, at the time of his biography on Mao, was a Research Associate at Harvard University's East Asian Research Center. His 1999 biography, published by Stanford Press, is both rich in detail and comprehensiveness and has numerous positive endorsements. Short's (2000) 782-page biography on Mao is so rich in prose that it stood out from the others in its comprehensiveness and attention to detail. Short's biography, published by Holt and Company in 2000, provided access to the latest information and interpretations about Mao.

As a companion to Gandhi's autobiography, Chadha's (1997) biography was selected because of the author's access to a plethora of primary and secondary sources relevant to Gandhi, the author was an Indian who had a "nodding acquaintance" (p. viii) with Gandhi, and its scholarly publisher John Wiley & Sons. The companion biography to MacArthur's autobiography was written by accomplished historian and biographer William Manchester, with 13 books to his credit by 1978, four of them biographies. Manchester (1978) fills 793 pages with dense and comprehensive details of MacArthur's life and time.

Blumenson's (1985) biography on Patton was endorsed both by reputed biographers and Patton's family members. Blumenson was one of America's leading military historians who also wrote the *Patton Papers* and had unprecedented access to various diaries, military papers and interviews with those close to Patton. With an almost clinical biography on Patton provided by Blumenson, a candid two-sided story, both personal and objective and well researched by Fred Ayer, Jr. (1964), Patton's nephew, was selected to bring a well-rounded perspective.

George Marshall was not prone to allow the limelight to be cast on him. As a matter of principle and respect to honor the privacy of those he worked with closely, Marshall was one of the few generals of WWII to refuse lavish offers for his memoirs and interviews. Mosely's (1982) biography was selected for his close work with the Marshall Foundation and experience with writing 22 historical narratives. Stoler (1989), at the time of his biography on Marshall, was a Fulbright lecturer, professor of history at the University of Vermont and visiting professor to the Naval War College. He had two other books on history to his credit, in addition to other publications and articles.

Prolific and accomplished historian Allan Nevins (1954, 1957, 1963) wrote a three-volume series totaling 1,910 pages on Henry Ford. Collaborating with various scholars and having access to records from the Ford Archives, Nevins narratives are cohesive, clear and comprehensive. Nevins' agenda to present insight about Ford, his accomplishments, vulnerabilities and the complex nature of his relationships with friends, family, work, the world and the context of the era in which he lived is evident in the balance and thorough treatment of the facts. With fewer choices, the second biography on Ford, while not as in depth, provided a comprehensive survey view of Ford's life span and was selected for the author's (Gelderman, 1981) self-proclaimed unhindered access to primary source documents.

A limitation in using published biographies is that the raw data has been through at least one filter of what is considered important and unimportant by the author. Such selectivity by the biographer or autobiographer may present a view of the data that may be more a commentary of the author than the subject (Carney, 1973). While published biographies and autobiographies consist of an additional layer of interpretation, they are subject to the same rules of interpretation and selectivity for any narrative. Whether evaluating primary data (life documents) versus secondary data (life stories), both are narrative accounts that follow the same rules of analysis and interpretation necessary to obtain meaningful conclusions (Riessman, 1993; Denzin, 1989; Lieblich, Tuval-Mashiach & Zilber, 1998).   Hermeneutics enables the researcher to contextualize the genre of the narrative to draw the appropriate conclusions, regardless of whether it is primary or secondary data.

A second limitation of using published biographies is the possibility of equating fame with leadership. By soliciting scholars to identify exemplary and competent leaders, it is reasonable to infer that scholars will discern the difference between popularity and substantive leadership. Gravitating to scholarly presses and serious biographers avoided the sensationalism sometimes associated with the public press and authors.

A third limitation with this approach is being restricted to those fortuitous enough to have a biography or autobiography to their credit. There are many notable leaders who do not have biographies to their credit and, yet, would yield just as valuable information about their development on the way to the top of their profession. However, by taking the "best of the best," in similar tradition of Collins and Porras (1997) and Bennis and Nanus (1985), it is reasonable to infer the principles will generalize to all types and levels of leaders. In addition, the top nominees for this study had at least two life narratives written about them. Thus, not one leader for this study was forfeited for lack of narratives.

For the purpose of this research, "competent" leaders were identified as *the most frequently cited people, in their respective field of study, that university scholars nominate as influential and widely recognized for their accomplishments and have at least two biographies or one biography and one autobiography to their credit.* The "exemplary" leaders were identified as *the most frequently cited people, in their respective field of study, that university scholars nominate as influential and widely recognized for their accomplishments, whose personal character and values make them truly exemplary and have at least two biographies or one biography and one autobiography to their credit.*

The data from the biographies and autobiographies was analyzed and evaluated for themes in the leader's development using narrative analysis, hermeneutics and grounded theory. Grounded theory, as developed by Strauss and Corbin (1998), posits that coding data according to conceptual themes will allow for synthesis of the data into an integrated theory. By continuously asking questions, making comparisons among the data and looking for multiple explanations, Strauss and Corbin assert groups of properties with various dimensions will emerge to reveal patterns. For example, a property revealed among the leaders being studied was the steady stream of significant others, or what was labeled prodigious patrons. The various dimensions of the prodigious patrons ranged from strangers to intimate friends and spouses.

Strauss and Corbin (1998) warn against entering the research with firm preconceived categories lest other categories be missed. The strategy is to enter the research with sensitivity to the theoretical issues so that subtleties to categories and their properties can emerge from the data. Initial central categories to understanding the process of leadership development include, but are not limited to, primary caregivers, childhood experiences, reported milestones, educational experiences, significant others, faith building experiences, and vocational experiences. Once a set of well-developed concepts, related through statements of relationships, are put together, a theory about the phenomenon in question emerges from the data.

Narrative analysis, as a method of inquiry, recognizes that narratives are representations of reality with a coherent structure and singular meaning. The assumption of narrative analysis is that a singular meaning is discernable from the storyteller. This is done by examining the various layers of meaning implicit in any message for congruency and coherency. The goals of narrative analysis, whether oral or written, are to discern from the layers of messages present in the life story the singular meaning as understood by the author of the story and discern the credibility of such interpretations. Like grounded theory, categories are identified from the content of the life story.

In the case of a biographer, the writer represents the life of the protagonist describing in detail the facts and facticities of the story. The storyteller arranges the data into categories and subcategories to convey a singular message. In narrative analysis research, it is sometimes obvious in identifying significant individuals, events and actions in the lives of the protagonists, which is exactly what is being looked for. Phrases such as "was influential," "this caused them to . . .," "without such . . .," "he attributed . . .," and so on help provide a composite of those influences that shaped the emerging leaders. There is sometimes more meaning in what is implicit versus what is explicit.

The author uses the surface meaning of words and the rules of syntax to convey the deeper meaning of what the facts and facticities represent. In response, the analyst uses rules of hermeneutics to analyze the surface meaning of words for the intended deeper meaning. Examining the framing (what and who is and is not included) in the narrative, the context of the message and the medium of the message provide clues to the author's credibility, biases and intended meaning.

What data the storyteller includes and excludes tests the credibility, significance and meaning of such categories. The context of the narrative or life story frames the significance and meaning of facts and facticities. Analyzing the context allows for the parts to inform the whole and for the whole to inform the parts. Evaluation of the words, tenor and mode provide additional clues to the meaning and significance of the narrative.

Along with writing style, word usage and order reveal emphasis and convey information about the commentator's agenda, biases and credibility. Writers prone to embellishment with use of superlatives erode their credibility. Biographers who provide only one perspective about their protagonist compromise their credibility and the reliability of the data with ignorance or bias influencing the story.

The tenor of communication reveals the quality of the relationship. The status of relationships is implied by the use of words. Two similar phrases "you need to . . ." and "we need to . . ." have a subtle yet potentially profound difference. The former statement to a colleague suggests the relationship is characterized by a real or perceived hierarchy. The latter statement reflects a more collegial relationship. Similar to the tenor, the mode evaluates for meaning beyond the medium of the words. Actual word usage (slang, sophisticated vocabulary, formal or informal titles), word emphasis and grammar communicate the rules of engagement and degrees of distance. For instance, the formality of language on the U.S. Senate floor conveys just as much about the nature of relationships and power structures as the words convey content. A written memo conveys different meta-messages than when the same content of the memo is communicated orally. A child addressing his or her parent as "mother" or "father" versus "mom" or "dad" suggests a more formal relationship.

Congruency and coherency from the context, the framing, the words, the tenor, and the mode of the spoken or written word reveal the intended meaning of the narrative. Evaluating what is included in the narrative and what is excluded provides additional clues for the reader of the reliability and validity of the narrative's veracity. The innocuous statement "A student purchased a book today" has a deeper meaning. What kind of student (a happy graduate, a sad undergraduate, a busy extension student), what type of school, what type of textbook, why was the textbook purchased today? How did the author of the statement know? A myriad of questions are raised from the surface meaning of words that aids the student of life narratives to discern the relevant and real facts and facticities.

Literal or objective hermeneutics brings a form of quality control to the interpretation of data, especially biographical or autobiographical material. The assumption of literal or objective hermeneutics is that while truth is known subjectively, it is metaphysically objective. Therefore, the goal of hermeneutics is to align as closely as possible the subjective interpretations to the objective reality of the phenomena being studied.

The hermeneutical spiral posits that the discovery of truth is a process of progressive revelation and a continual refinement of one's interpretations. The precise meaning is discerned by tentative conclusions informing previous conclusions that, in turn, inform future conclusions until the data fits tightly together. Searching for coherence and congruency in the text leads to conclusions that approximate the objective reality and may even lead to a one-to-one correspondence with the objective reality. Thus, it follows from hermeneutics that some conclusions are more accurate than other conclusions. Like narrative analysis, congruency and coherence among the framing, the context and the medium lead to valid conclusions about the messages and lessons in the narrative.

Hermeneutics and narrative analysis are tools that allow for a careful search for the author's intended meaning and veracity by exploring below the surface structure of the words. Implementing the various methods outlined allows for drawing conclusions about the shaping influences that facilitated individuals to emerge as leaders.

Sample Selection

Professors, Associate Professors and Assistant Professors in Educational Administration, Business Management, Military Science, and Religious Studies were contacted via e-mail, obtained from their respective University's web page. A total of 5,060 e-mails were sent. Appendix A contains the e-mail correspondence. Nine hundred thirteen came back as undeliverable mail. Another 105 returned with the recipient stating they were not in the position to respond for various reasons (i.e., they were either not an expert, retired or for various reasons uncomfortable participating with the study.) A total of 614 usable responses were received. Based on the 4,147 e-mails that were sent and presumably received; the total response rate was 17.3% and the response rate for usable replies was 15%.

The breakdown of e-mails sent and received in business, education, military science, political science, and religious studies are listed respectively in Tables 1, 2, 3, 4 and 5.

Table 1 - Business Responses

	Professors	Associate	Assistant	Total
Originally Sent	748	420	381	1549
Undeliverable	<208>	<90>	<89>	<387>
Delivered	540	330	292	1162
Received #/ %	58/ 11%	20/ 6%	23/ 8% (2)*	103/ 9%

*Two unsolicited e-mail replies were received as a result of my original solicitation being forwarded to them.

Table 2 - Education Responses

	Professors	Associate	Assistant	Total
Originally Sent	604	349	294	1247
Undeliverable	<96>	<48>	<30>	<174>
Delivered	508	301	264	1073
Received #/ %	48/ 9%	58/ 19%	40/ 15%	146/ 18%

Table 3 - Military Science Responses

	Military Officers*
Originally Sent	311
Undeliverable	<59>
Delivered	252
Received #/ %	77/ 31%

*Military officers instructing in ROTC programs were contacted regardless of academic rank.

Table 4 - Political Science Responses

	Professors	Associate	Assistant	Total
Originally Sent	812	424	368	1604
Undeliverable	<123>	<65>	<47>	<235>
Delivered	689	359	321	1369
Received #/ %	139/ 20%	51/ 14%	45/ 14%	235/ 17%

Table 5 - Religious Studies Responses

	Professors	Associate	Assistant	Total
Originally Sent	170	110	69	349
Undeliverable	<38>	<11>	<9>	<58>
Delivered	132	99	60	291
Received #/ %	29/ 22%	17/ 17%	7/ 12%	53/ 18%

Given the nature of the number of nominations received for education and religious studies, the leaders of this prosopography were limited to business, military and politics. The top nominees for religious studies, with the exception of Martin Luther King, had more nominations in the exemplary category than in the competent category. Basically, as tentatively expected, most of the religious leaders were considered exemplary and, as a result, no meaningful comparison group was available among the religious leaders.

The reverse was true for the top nominees for the educational leaders. None of the top nominees for educational leaders received a higher number of exemplary nominations making it difficult to obtain a comparison group. In addition, the response from the 146 e-mails nominating educational leaders resulted in 418 different nominations, representing very little consensus on who are considered the most influential leaders in education. In contrast, the responses in the other fields converged to provide some sense of consensus on who are the influential leaders. For business, 103 replies nominated 174 different leaders. For the military, 77 replies nominated 107 different leaders. For politics, 235 replies nominated 183 leaders. For religious studies, 53 replies nominated 107 leaders.

The two exemplary business leaders and the two competent business leaders were Jack Welch, Sam Walton, Henry Ford and Bill Gates, respectfully. The two exemplary political leaders and the two competent political leaders were Franklin Roosevelt, Mohandas Gandhi, Adolph Hitler and Mao Tse-tung, respectfully. The two exemplary military leaders and the two competent military leaders were George Marshall, Colin Powell, Douglas MacArthur and George Patton, respectfully.

Table 6 lists the date of birth and death of the exemplary and competent leaders in alphabetical order.

Table 6 - List of Leaders

Competent Leaders			Exemplary Leaders		
Name	DOB	DOD	Name	DOB	DOD
Military			Military		
MacArthur, D.	Jan. 26, 1880	April 5, 1964	Marshall, G	Dec. 30, 1880	Oct. 16, 1959
Patton, G.	Nov. 11, 1885	Dec. 21, 1945	Powell, C.	April 5, 1937	---
Politics			Politics		
Hitler, A.	April 20, 1889	April 30, 1945	Gandhi, M.	Oct. 2, 1869	Jan. 3, 1948
Mao, T.	Dec. 26, 1893	Sept. 9, 1976	Roosevelt, F.	Jan. 30, 1882	April 12, 1945
Business			Business		
Ford, H.	July 30, 1863	April 7, 1947	Walton, S.	March 24, 1918	April 6, 1992
Gates, B.	Oct. 28, 1955	---	Welch, J.	Nov. 19, 1935	---

With the exception of Bill Gates, all the leaders were alive at the same time, albeit a brief period of overlap, and shared the effects of World War II, albeit on different continents. The average life span of our leaders, up to August of 2004, is 69.3 and 71.8 for the competent and exemplary, respectfully. Collectively, the 12 leaders represent 847 years of experiences and influences from which to glean lessons.

Seven Influences

The competent and exemplary individuals had in common many formative life experiences and background characteristics that contributed to their emergence as reputable and influential leaders. The biographies and autobiographies discussed critical people and events that served as defining points in the leader's rise to influential accomplishments. Seven properties or categories were consistent among the biographies and autobiographies. Involved parents, happy childhood experiences, meaningful formal and informal education, a steady stream of prodigious patrons, friendly critics and adversaries, a series of successful mini-apprenticeships, and a favorable fate served important roles in leaders emerging to a position of influence and accomplishment. In addition, the exemplary leaders had a qualitatively different experience with their parents and the caliber of prodigious patrons that distinguished them all the more. Appendix B illustrates the different categories with their respective dimensions and properties.

What follows is an explanation of each category.

Involved Parents

A common denominator among all the leaders was a strong attachment and involvement with their mothers. For each leader, the mother is reported to be the early strong influence on them. Sarah Roosevelt structured a variety of experiences for Franklin Roosevelt (FDR) during his childhood, while continually reminding FDR of the principle of *noblesse oblige*; responsibility comes with privilege. A curriculum of nannies, private education, and travels abroad served to place high expectations on FDR. While she resisted FDR's involvement with politics, Sarah Roosevelt remained a confidant and financial supporter of FDR until her death in 1941, at the start of Roosevelt's third term as President. Sarah took seriously her responsibility to raise an educated country gentleman squire who would be involved in works for the public.

Gandhi's impression of his mother is "that of saintliness" (Chadha, 1997, p. 5). It was her modeling of deep religious values that provided Gandhi a sense of loyalty to an oath made to her of his abstaining from women, meat and wine while studying in England. This proved to be a precursor to the deepening of Gandhi's religious observances.

Welch reports that as a senior in high school, his mother forced her way into her son's locker room after a display of poor sportsmanship on the hockey rink following a loss.

> She went right for me, grabbing the top of my uniform. 'You punk!' she shouted in my face. 'If you don't know how to lose, you'll never know how to win. If you don't know this, you shouldn't be playing.' I was mortified – in front of my friends – but what she said never left me. (Welch, 2001, p. 3)

Welch's mother was always making teaching moments. Welch attributes much of his self-confidence to the many positive messages and high standards imposed on him by his mother.

After MacArthur graduated from high school in Texas, MacArthur's mother made special arrangements for her and Douglas to live in Milwaukee. In Milwaukee, MacArthur would receive medical treatment for curvature of the spine and tutoring for the West Point exams. In addition, they moved to Milwaukee to take advantage of family contacts for Douglas to secure an appointment to West Point, which he failed to get a year earlier for the above reasons.

Walton's mother relocated the family to Columbia, Missouri during Sam's high school year for better opportunities and to increase Sam's competitiveness to get into the universities. Sam reports of his mother as having high ambitions for her children, she read much to her children and loved education. Sam attributes his passion to his mother's example and her hopes for him instilled success.

In an interview with Parade magazine, Powell (1995) shared:

> My parents, I said, did not recognize their own strengths. It was nothing they said or taught us, I recalled. It was the way they lived their lives, I said. If the values seem correct or relevant, the children will follow the values. I had been shaped not by preaching, but by example, by moral osmosis. Banana Kelly, the embracing warmth of an extended family, St. Margaret's Church, and let's weave in the Jamaican roots and a little calypso – all provided an enviable send-off on life's journey. (p. 37)

Mary Ford (Henry Ford's mother) was an industrious wife and mother who not only taught Henry to read, but also that "wrong-doing carries its own punishment" (Nevins, 1954, p. 51), and a dedication to order and cleanliness.

The influence of Ford's mother is evident when Henry states, "I have tried to live my life as my mother would have wished. I believe I have done, as far as I could, just what she hoped for me" (Nevins, 1954, p. 51).

For Marshall, "clearly she [Marshall's mother] was the most important person in his childhood and by his own recollection a 'constant and lasting influence on my life'" (Stoler, 1989, p. 5). She was his affectionate confidante later admitting, "that his mother spoiled him" (Stoler, 1989, p. 5).

What these examples illustrate is that a mother's attention to her children in guiding and shaping their experiences and providing encouragement lays the foundation and support structures for future abilities and dispositions in life. While the biographies and autobiographies do not contain much detail describing exactly what these mothers did to be so influential, it appears they were attentive, involved in the routine of their children's lives and communicated high expectations.

Five out of the six exemplary leaders and four out of six competent leaders had strong support from both sets of parents. While Marshall, Hitler and Mao perceived their father's as aloof and critical, each father still provided financial and personal assistance for his child in the early transition points. Hitler's father, a philanderer, sired Adolf while his third wife, to be, was his mistress. Mao considered his father mean and stingy. While Mao was the only one to grow up to hate his father; his father, none-the-less, sacrificed to have Mao receive an elementary and secondary education. Marshall's father organized a letter campaign for George to be allowed to take the examination and become an officer in the expanding army.

Parents played a pivotal role and are acknowledged in the various biographies and autobiographies for their special influence. For Gates, Wallace and Erickson (1992) write:

> Gifted children – those with IQs near or above the genius level – sometimes grow up to be socially inept, due to limited childhood interactions and experiences. Bill and Mary Gates were determined to see that this didn't happen to their son. They tried to expose him to as many opportunities and experiences as possible. (p. 12)

Patton's father read much to George and told and read stories of heroes and family accomplishments in order to shape Patton's aspirations.

A dynamic in MacArthur and Patton was a sense of duty to be great given the family lineage of great people and heroic soldiers who would become their cloud of witnesses. The focus of their indulging parents was for their children to be great, in contrast to Sarah Roosevelt whose emphasis was on doing great things. MacArthur, Patton and Roosevelt were very much the focus of their parents' affections and energies, yet Roosevelt did not emerge as eccentric and with as frequent self-serving behavior as MacArthur and Patton. Roosevelt's mother continually reminded FDR of the obligations that come from nobility. Patton's and MacArthur's parents continually discussed the importance of becoming great, which was a driving force throughout much of their careers. Of MacArthur's relationship with his mother, Manchester (1978) writes:

> A mama's boy who reached his fullest dimensions in following maternal orders to be mercilessly ambitious. Pinky MacArthur moved to the U.S. Military Academy when he enrolled there – from Cranny's Hotel she could see the lamp in her son's room and tell whether or not he was studying – and later she mortified him by writing ludicrous letters to his superiors, demanding that he be promoted. (p. 4)

With the exception of Hitler's parents, the message given by the parents was one of expectation of doing something good with one's life. Patton and MacArthur grew up haunted by the ghosts of fame in their family tree, and so, they viewed themselves as special stock, duty-bound to become famous. This selfish ambition surfaced frequently and seems to explain some of the eccentric, attention getting behavior of both Generals. If they did not get a promotion, honor or recognition they thought they deserved, it became a point of sulking and protest to their superiors. Patton frequently expressed disappointment in the war's end or that his age might make him miss additional wars, thus not having a context to showcase his abilities and achieve fame.

Undoubtedly, the parents played a prodigious role in the life of each leader. One difference between the parents of the exemplary and that of the competent leaders was the degree of family devotion to formal church activities or religious practices. Gandhi, Welch, Walton, Roosevelt, Marshall and Powell came from families where religion and church involvement were an important tradition in the family and are referenced accordingly in the sources. Words such as "religious," "devout," "active," "important," and "members" describe the references made to the parents of the exemplary leaders in relation to their religious observances.

This inherited faith would serve as an anchor and, at some critical times, a returning point for strength and guidance. This is illustrated when Roosevelt was first diagnosed with polio. "After a week his temperature dropped and his spirits rose. His buoyancy and strong religious faith reasserted themselves, and he felt he must have been shattered and spared for a purpose beyond his knowledge" (Freidel, 1990, p. 41). In contrast, the biographies and autobiographies of the competent leaders made passing reference to meaningful family involvement in church or religious activities. While Mao's mother was a devout Buddhist and Hitler's mother was a devout catholic, the practice of religious observances was isolated to the individual members versus a family affair.

The principle of at least one parent connecting with the child, knowing their strengths, weaknesses, potentials, and guiding their experiences, thoughts and emotions is attributed by the leaders as a determinative influence. In each case, at least one parent is responsible for planting the seed of confidence and ambition. Also appearing to increase the likelihood of developing exemplary leaders, formal religious involvement serves as a starting point for some sort of moral compass to develop that distinguishes the leaders as exemplary. The religious foundation and moral voice served as a strange attractor, a center reference point in which actions and decisions were kept in a relative and patterned range amongst the competing demands, values and dilemmas associated with leadership.

A Happy Childhood

Childhood for our leaders was considered relatively supportive and stable characterized by play, chores and school. With the exception of minor trauma in the childhood of some of the leaders, they still had enough positive experiences to emerge from their childhood with ambition and a sense of self-efficacy. While Mao's father could be mean and Walton's parents regularly argued loudly, both leaders report pleasant memories from their childhood. Marshall was awkward and teased by his siblings and peers. Even though Hitler was orphaned by age 12 and was a loner, his early childhood was still portrayed as a stable and supportive period, as it was for all of the leaders.

Ford had a nice childhood, despite detesting farm work. At the age of 12, 1876 became a pivotal year for Ford. First, there was the tragedy of his mother's death. Thanks to the determination and resilience of his father, the work on the farm and the raising of five children (the four year old Robert, the youngest of the 6, died), the Fords prospered. Second, three additional events happened in Ford's informal education that spurred his fascination with machinery. For the first time he saw a self-propelled steam engine. Then he received a watch, which he took apart and rebuilt numerous times. His father also traveled to the Centennial Exposition of 1876 and told Henry all about the latest inventions and machines. These activities all the more fueled Henry's ambitions to leave home to gain experience in the machine shops of Detroit. Always experimenting with mechanical things in school and on the farm, upon finishing school at the age of 17, he left for Detroit to work for the Michigan Car Company.

Walton's image of life was forever influenced by the depression and seeing the tragedies that came with his father's job of foreclosing on farms. Yet, at the same time, Walton knew of his parent's support and safety, growing up in a relatively financially stable home in the depression.

With the exception of Hitler, our leaders lived comfortable lives, with none being subject to poverty during their early years. Granted, some families were forced to be frugal and lacked discretionary means, but basic needs were never in jeopardy of being met. Even Hitler had an orphan's pension that allowed for material comforts and the opportunity to pursue additional education, if he had been found an acceptable student.

For the most part, the children grew up in homogenous communities with rules and values consistent with those of their parents. Such homogeneity and closeness of the immediate community reinforced the values taught at home. Powell and Welch discuss the closeness of the neighborhood acting as surrogate parents. Gandhi's caste system served a familial function. As children, they had the luxury of play and participating in the family chores. Walton excelled in school athletics. Welch and Powell played many neighborhood games in the streets of their youth. Roosevelt, while he didn't excel in team sports, was still able to play and was an active child. From sports and play, they describe learning teamwork, diligence and how to be active agents in their fate. For Marshall, his childhood has been referred to as "relatively unremarkable" (Stoler, 1989, p. 6).

For Powell, Roth (1993) writes:

> Growing up, Colin Powell was surrounded by a close net of neighborhood family friends and actual and fictive kin – West Indian 'aunts,' 'uncle,' and 'cousins' who saw his every move and made certain that he toed the line. This extended family and social network cared for its youth by both encouraging and challenging them. Social pressure to conform was only exceeded by an expectation that the immigrant second-generation was marked by achievement. (p. 33)

MacArthur had sort of a frontier childhood, the son of a distinguished army officer, frequently relocating to various military outposts. This provided opportunities to play in the context of war stories floating around the outposts. At the age of eight, he relocated to Leavenworth and got to play with children his own age.

Surprisingly, not many details of childhood were provided in the biographies and autobiographies. Nothing of the childhood experiences emerged that helped distinguish the exemplary leaders from the competent leaders. Both groups had similar composition of families of varied social economic status and geographical locations. What can be inferred is that a supportive and secure childhood lends itself to successful childhood play and experiences, which for the most part germinated the seeds of confidence to that of ability and industry. In addition, to raise children to grow up to be healthy adults, it appears a village of active participants concerned for the welfare of each child helps tremendously.

Formal and Informal Education

The leaders in this study benefited much from either their formal or informal education. Every leader was well read and was exposed to a variety of writers and thinkers. With the exception of Hitler and Ford, the leaders were able to receive post-secondary formal education. Of the remaining ten leaders, Gates was the only one not to earn a university degree. It is interesting to note that among the exemplary leaders, not one considered themselves an exceptional student during their secondary and undergraduate work. With the exception of Welch, they did not graduate from college near the top of their class. They were capable, but, for the most part, considered average academically among their peers.

After private tutors and home school, at the age of 14, Roosevelt went to Groton School, which was an Episcopal school with a strong purpose. Rector Endicott Peabody, who was the founder and headmaster at Groton stated, "If some Groton boys do not enter political life and do something for our land, it won't be because they have not been urged" (Freidel, 1990, p. 8). Peabody would be a paragon of virtue and strength for Roosevelt. Forty years after graduating from Groton, Roosevelt wrote to Peabody, "I count it among the blessing of my life that it was given to me in formative years to have the privilege of your guiding hand" (Burns, 1984, p. 16). When Peabody died in 1944, Roosevelt wrote his widow that the "whole tone of things is going to be different from now on, for I have leaned on the Rector in all these many years far more than most people know. . . "(Burns, 1984, p. 468). Roosevelt's Groton experience exposed him to another role model in which he would set out to emulate. "While Roosevelt was at Groton he also first fell under the spell of his remote cousin Theodore Roosevelt" (Freidel, 1990, p. 10).

While not an exceptional student, Roosevelt was able to experience curricular and co-curricular success, which became a source of validation as a capable and competent person. Freidel (1990) states:

> While Groton gave Roosevelt an impetus toward public service, Harvard provided him with some of the ideas he would bring to it. As was true of the young socialites in that era of the gentlemanly C grade, scholarship was near the bottom of priorities. Nevertheless, Roosevelt enrolled in substantial courses, many of them in economics and history, in which he was exposed to the new progressive concepts of the role of government in regulating the economy. . . . Yet it would be easy to exaggerate the influence of the brilliant faculty upon Roosevelt. The few examples of his undergraduate writing that have survived are mediocre and uncritical. Extracurricular activities and social life were so much more important to Roosevelt that the wonder is his receiving passing grades, not his failure to dazzle his professors. (p. 10)

While at Harvard his involvement in various co-curricular activities brought much connection and pride, especially being president of the Harvard Crimson for a semester of his senior year. "What Franklin D. Roosevelt learned at Harvard that would be of later use in politics came less from the classroom than from extracurricular activities" (Freidel, 1990, p. 11). While at Columbia Law School he was a "C" student and even failed two classes. Once he passed the bar exam, Roosevelt did not complete his course work to earn his L.L.B degree.

Gandhi did mediocre in his studies, barely passing the matriculation examinations for college. Gandhi considered himself a decent student but more, because he was conscientious toward his studies. The kindness of one teacher put him to shame. "I could not disregard my teacher's affection" (Gandhi, 1948, p. 30). One teacher in particular sought Gandhi out and encouraged him to study the language of his religion. He would be available to help if he had difficulty. Gandhi writes of him:

> Today I cannot but think with gratitude of Krishnashankar Panday. For if I had not acquired the little Sanskrit that I learned then, I should have found it difficult to take any interest in our sacred books. In fact I deeply regret that I was not able to acquire a more thorough knowledge of the language. (Gandhi, 1948, p. 30)

Gandhi first enrolled in Samaldas College for a short term. Gandhi (1948) writes of his first experiment with college:

> I went, but found myself entirely at sea. Everything was difficult. I could not follow, let alone take [sic] interest in, the professors' lectures. It was no fault of theirs. The professors in the College were regarded as first-rate. But I was so raw. At the end of first term, I returned home. (p. 52)

At the suggestion of a family friend, Gandhi went to London for three years to study to become a barrister at law. In those three years, he was exposed to ideas, discussion groups and thinking that began to enthuse and inform his worldview. He read *Song of the Blessed*, which became part of his daily devotional reading. He read the *Bible* and Carlyle's *Heroes and Hero Worship*. Gandhi was able to pass the bar after twelve terms. Gandhi reports that he always enjoyed the affection of his teachers, and that appeared to be a sustaining force in his continuing with his education. The leisure of being a student afforded Gandhi opportunities, via reading and discussions, to develop his embryonic convictions of religious and political practices.

After passing the bar, Gandhi still felt fear and helplessness to practice law. A friend shared, "I understand your trouble. Your general reading is meagre. You have no knowledge of the world, a *sine qua non* for a vakil" (Gandhi, 1948, p. 107). That comment became an impetus for Gandhi to read broadly and study thoroughly.

Marshall was a poor student, apparently, in part, because of poor preparation. His great-aunt harshly and rigidly structured his early lessons so that when it came time to enter public school he was soured and ill prepared for the experience. As a result, he hated school. Once he decided he would be a soldier, he headed for the Virginia Military Institute (VMI). Enthused with a new purpose, he soon excelled while still a mediocre student academically. Marshall was able, with effort, to be 19th in his class of 47 (Stoler, 1989).

At the age of 26, after four years of reputable service, Marshall reported to the Staff College at Fort Leavenworth. Marshall distinguished himself academically, due in part to the new educational system of progressiveness (Stoler, 1989). While he had to work extremely hard, it was at Leavenworth that Marshall "learned how to learn" (Stoler, 1989, p. 23). Because of his success at Leavenworth, the board unanimously selected him to remain as an instructor, which he did for two years.

While Powell (1995) writes, "thanks to an accelerated school program rather than any brilliance on my part, I graduated from Morris High School two months short of my seventeenth birthday" (p. 20). Even though he graduated early from high school, he states that he "had not yet excelled at anything" (p. 20). Choosing engineering as a major because of the opportunities versus an affinity, Powell enrolled at the City College of New York (CCNY). While not lasting long in the engineering program, he came across the ROTC program and immediately discovered a niche in which he could identify with and excel. Powell graduated from CCNY with barely above a C average, having A's in his military subjects and B's in geology courses, which was his major. Of his experience at CCNY, Powell (1995) reflectfully writes:

> I also owe an unpayable debt to the New York City public education system. I typified the students that CCNY was created to serve, the sons and daughters of the inner city, the poor, the immigrant. Many of my college classmates had the brainpower to attend Harvard, Yale, or Princeton. What they lacked was money and influential connections. . . . I have made clear that I was not great shakes as a scholar. . . . Yet, even this C-average student emerged from CCNY prepared to write, think, and communicate effectively and equipped to compete against students from colleges that I could never have dreamed of attending. (p. 37)

Welch's informal education began early, as his father, a train conductor, would bring home various newspapers discarded from travelers on the train. Welch was turned down for a Naval ROTC scholarship and with it went his hopes off attending Dartmouth or Columbia. Welch (2001) was a capable student and reports:

> I was a good student who worked hard for his grades, but no one
> would have accused me of being brilliant. So I applied to the
> University of Massachusetts at Amherst, the state school, where the
> tuition was fifty bucks a semester. For less than $1,000, including
> room and board, I could get a degree. (p. 14)

He credits his professors with making him something of their pet project
and was encouraged by them to go to graduate school. Welch (2001) saw it as a
blessing that he did not get the Navy ROTC scholarship and ended up at the
University of Massachusetts. "I was one of the university's two best students
graduating with a degree in chemical engineering. If I'd gone to MIT, I might
have been in the middle of the pile" (p. 15). At graduate school at the University
of Illinois in Champaign, liking his faculty, and with the help of faculty mentors
and hard work, he earned a Ph.D. in Chemical Engineering in three years,
commenting he was far from the program's resident genius. Welch benefited
much from his education believing his degree in chemical engineering prepared
him well for a career in business and cultivated an appreciation for
understanding the complexity associated with running a dynamic organization.

Walton was a campus leader both in high school and college. In high
school, he was involved in student government, he played football and
basketball and joined a variety of campus clubs. At Hickman High School, "I
got involved in just about everything. I wasn't what you'd call a gifted student,
but I worked really hard and made the honor roll" (Walton, 1992, p. 17). In
college "he became an officer of the fraternity he joined; president of an ROTC
club; president of the senior men's honor society; a member of the governing
board of the college's yearbook; president of his Bible class; and president of his
senior class" (Ortega, 1998, p. 21). In addition, Sam delivered newspapers and
waited on tables while earning his degree in Business. Such a wealth of varied
experiences helped Sam refine his natural talents and inclinations and prepared
him for his job with J.C. Penney's immediately following his graduation from
the University of Missouri.

Each exemplary leader considered their formal education valuable in
providing various experiences and preparation for their careers. With the
exception of Marshall, who at the age of 17 decided to be a soldier, following
high school graduation, the exemplary leaders did not select the career they
ended up in. In addition, these leaders emerged out of the ranks of average
students with average performance to that of outstanding performance. With
higher education competing for only the "brightest," many potential exemplary
leaders may be missed.

In addition, our exemplary leaders benefited, directly and indirectly, from a
college experience. Keeping higher education affordable for the most people
possible seems a mandate to increase the likelihood of developing additional
exemplary leaders. Not only is it important to make the experiences affordable,

but to provide the right type of experience. Co-curricular activities and surrogate parenting on behalf of the faculty and support staff, versus just dispensing of knowledge, provides a continuous context for personal and professional development, a source of encouragement, and a sense of belonging for the leaders in this crucial stage of their development.

For the competent leaders, it is a mixed bag of results when it comes to viewing their academic experiences. Ford learned to read from his mother prior to attending the Scotch Settlement School at the age of seven and a half. It was here Ford was influenced by the McGuffey readers, evident "when he went to great expense to reissue and distribute the McGuffey readers, and used them in the schools he established at Greenfield Village" (Nevins, 1954, p. 46). Finishing school at the age of 16, instead of pursuing college like some of his school friends, Ford went to work in Detroit.

Ford's lack of a college education would plague him in his years of success, even influencing where he would live. He purposefully built his mansion in seclusion and apart from Detroit's educated elite, lest he embarrass himself. In addition, his uneducated mind would later be a disservice to him and, eventually, be a piece of the puzzle that lead to a hardening of his critical and autocratic temperament and isolation. In a libel suit against the Chicago Tribune, Ford attempted to portray himself as a patriot, but frequently misspoke and was confused on the facts. The attorney for the Tribune took advantage of Ford's academic deficits only to draw more attention to Ford's ignorance. The Tribune went to great lengths to satire Ford as a means of vindication and influencing public opinion on the case.

In addition, Ford's lack of confidence in his intellectual abilities, made him more vulnerable and easily swayed by his advisors and confidants. His controversy with the "Jewish Problem," the Peace Ship, controlling of Edsel and anti-union activities in the 1920s was more consistent of his advisors thoughts than his own. Nevins (1957) sums it up when he writes:

> Meanwhile, his early environment laid penalties on the industrialist. Like other untutored men, he has a suspicion of the uncomprehendable, a susceptibility to bad counsel, and a tenacious hold on prejudices. His antagonism to Wall Street may have owed something to Populist influences and to his anxieties in the 1920-1922: but surely three fourths of it was trust of what he did not understand. His hostility to the "international Jew" was mainly founded on ignorance. Part of it was ideological, but it was the ideology of misinformation, not malice. (p. 618)

Gates, a genius, read through a whole encyclopedia set as a child. He flourished at Lakeside Private School in Seattle where a classmate said, "even the dumb kids are smart" (Wallace and Erickson, 1992, p. 19). Lakeside was able to match a curriculum with his abilities and interests with teachers who understood how to work with the eccentricities of the gifted. At a wealthy private school, Gates was afforded the rare opportunity as a student to have share time on a computer, a rarity in the 1960s. Gates would attend Harvard out of honor to his parents but would be a perfunctory student. With his Micro-Soft Company demanding his talent and time, Gates left Harvard without completing the requirements for his degree.

Hitler continually struggled in his academics and was held back on two occasions, eventually dropping out of school. He was denied admission to the Academy of Fine Art, which was a path for his hopes of becoming an artist. Rejected and lonely and now living in Vienna, Hitler came across anti-Semitic literature in addition to a periodical devoted to the promotion of the Aryan league. This would become the new focus of his readings. Hitler's learning came from informal sources. Fest (1992) states:

> From this and other influences, such as the newspaper articles and cheap pamphlets that Hitler himself mentioned as early sources of his knowledge, some scholars have concluded that his worldview was the product of a perverted subculture opposed to bourgeois culture. (p. 37)

It was not until Hitler hooked up with radical socialists that he started assimilating various ideas from revolutionary thinkers through reading what was available. While in prison, Hitler was to formulate his thinking with additional reading and write *Mein Kampf* (My Struggle). Hitler referred to his imprisonment as his "university at state expense" (Fest, 1992, p. 218).

Mao appeared to have a propensity for school. At the age of eight Mao was able to leave the farm work and attend school in the village. He found the system of rote learning tedious and harsh. For the first two years "he spent his days from sunrise to dusk memorizing, copying and reciting moralistic phrases like, 'Diligence has merit; play yields no profit', having no idea what they meant" (Short, 2000, p. 26). The following two years of his education evolved to discussing the meaning of various Confucian thoughts, which were to inform his future thinking and debates. While attending school, Mao saw two decapitated heads of rebel peasants posted on the city's gate. Uprisings as such and the savage treatment of the rebels were a point of discussion in the school and an early and vivid introduction to Mao's revolutionary thinking.

At the age of 13, Mao had to return to his father's field and take a hiatus from his formal education. At the age of 16, Mao was able to convince his father to have him return to school in a neighboring village. This boarding experience brought Mao into contact with many wealthy students who treated Mao as not one of their own, but rather as a son of a farmer. It was here at the Upper Primary School that Mao was exposed to the revolutionary and reform writings and ideas taking place in China at the time. He enjoyed reading broadly. Terrill

(1999) states, "his success at books, consolation for his social unhappiness, was itself a coin with two sides. It made some pupils despise his narrow zeal all the more" (p. 49). Reading *Great Heroes of the World,* Mao became open to a world of possibilities for China and how he might have a role.

Mao left Upper Primary School in the spring of 1911 to try his academic prowess at another school in the large capital city of eight hundred thousand people. It was here, as a 17-year-old, he saw a newspaper for the first time and learned about current events. After four weeks in his new school, Mao was so caught up in the energies of the nationalist movement that he enlisted in the Hunan unit of the revolutionary army (Terrill, 1999). Thinking the revolution had come to an end, in 1912, he resigned from the army in order to return to his studies.

Not finding a school to his liking, Mao spent the next six months on an aggressive course of self-study in the Hunan Province Library. Mao "would later judge this half year among books to be a high point of his life" (Terrill, 1999, p. 54). Needing to make a living, Mao noticed an advertisement for a teacher's training school with no fees to pay. He enrolled into the new First Teacher's Training School (FTTS) where he zealously read broadly and deeply both western and eastern scholars. Mao was also elected head of the Students' Society, responsible for organizing extra-curricular activities at the college. Mao graduated third from FTTS in 1918 earning a teaching diploma. "Like others in his circle, he was socially adrift, a dissenter, and a bundle of mental contradictions" (Terrill, 1999, p. 61).

Mao found a mentor in one of his professors, Professor Yang. Along with a small group of students, Mao would frequent the professor's house to discuss current events and the cultivation of virtues. When Mao's professor and mentor from FTTS took a position at Peking University, Mao, with the recommendation of his mentor, was able to secure a job in the periodical room at the Peking University Library. Terrill (1999) says it well when he states that "the Chinese Revolution began in a library. A doctrine was needed to give direction to the formless revolt against the old" (p. 67).

With his job in the library, Mao could read as much as he wanted. It was in the library he came across Marx and Lenin. In 1919, after participating in various revolutionary groups active in Peking he left to visit Confucius's grave and eventually returned to Changsha and became a leader in the new cultural movement enveloping China. Mao would fuel the revolution with speeches and writings that were very much a product of his formal and informal education.

MacArthur, as a son of a military officer, relocated relatively frequently and had different formal educational experiences. His father was extremely well read, leaving 4,000 books to MacArthur. At age six his father was transferred to Leavenworth where MacArthur began second grade and was now surrounded by kids his own age. At age nine he was transferred to Washington to Force Public

School. "His academic performance continued to be indifferent" (Manchester, 1978, p. 44). In 1893, at 13, he was relocated to San Antonio. MacArthur entered the academy, later to be known as the Texas Military Institute. The academy was founded by an Episcopalian bishop, and it was here that MacArthur would say he started (Manchester, 1978). He became an outstanding student and athlete earning various accolades and becoming the valedictorian of the class of 1897.

In spite of his success, MacArthur was not able to secure a West Point appointment nor was he able to pass a preliminary physical. Mrs. MacArthur and Douglas relocated to Milwaukee because family connections would allow Douglas to obtain medical correction of his curvature of the spine and be in a better position to gain a congressional appointment. In 1898 MacArthur earned the congressional appointment by his placement on the competitive exam and soon after passed the required physical. At the age of 19, he was headed to West Point. It was at West Point, under his mother's watchful eye and daily encouragement (she relocated to West Point and remained living there throughout MacArthur's tenure) and initial influence of the upperclassmen that helped MacArthur finish first in his class.

Patton's education began early with his father reading to him and telling him many stories about great relatives and other men of glory. The almost 12-year-old dyslexic Patton became enrolled in Stephen Clark's School for Boys in Pasadena, with approximately 25 students.

School was difficult for Patton. As Blumenson (1985) records:

> He struggled constantly to deal with his reading and writing disability, which hindered his learning. Acquiring knowledge demanded intense concentration and diligence. The deficiency led to occasional humiliation, for his schoolmates mocked his errors at the blackboard and his reading aloud. His parents' love, their warm support, sustained his spirits and fueled his determination to succeed. (p. 34)

At the age of 17, Patton declared that he would become a soldier with hopes of going to West Point. Since the competitive exams held by the sponsoring senator or congressman would probably preclude Patton from earning a nomination, the route through the Virginia Military Institute (VMI) was selected which would connect Patton to his roots and help him mature. His dyslexia caused some problems, however, requiring him to be all the more painstakingly thorough in reading and writing. In the meantime, Patton was able to take the exam and earn his senator's nomination for West Point, thanks to much lobbying by his father.

At West Point, Blumenson (1985) states:

> . . . . his studies gave him much concern. He worried constantly about his academic standing. Reciting and writing at the blackboard in class were very difficult. He felt worthless and stupid much of the time, for he had to work hard for everything, and he envied his classmates who made good grades with much less work. (p. 49)

In spite of passing his academic requirements in the middle of his class, his academic struggles made him think of himself as incompetent, as he was already prone to self-deprecation. What sustained him were his parents who understood his difficulties and Beatrice (his future bride). The accoutrements that came with life at West Point (command over the plebes, co-curricular activities) provided the outlet for Patton's energies and confirmation of his ability to be a soldier. In the spring of his fourth year, he was appointed adjutant of the corps of cadets, a position that fulfilled his desires and opportunities to shine. Patton graduated in five years with an athletic letter and as an accomplished swordsman and an expert sharpshooter.

Unsurprisingly, formal and informal education played a strategic role in the formation of our leaders. Educators will do well to recognize that these average inclined students revealed much potential. For most, the high school years and college years were a catalyst for the student gaining knowledge and skills that would serve each leader. Providing a breadth of co-curricular activities, personal involvement and mentoring of the students appear to go a long way in having students maximize their opportunities and find niches in which to prosper. When education had a perceived purpose, was meaningful and relevant to our leaders, they became enthused for learning. Formal and informal learning equipped the leaders with a deep well of necessary knowledge and skills with which to draw upon in their practice of leadership. Through their education, each leader was exposed to a broader world that became formative in their thinking and worldview. Education planted, watered and tended to the growing plants, with the leaders having the luxury to devote portions of their life to study and expand their horizons.

Prodigious Patrons

Prodigious patrons are people who, almost with a providential timing, and unwittingly at the time, become strategic catalysts for the leader to make it to the next plateau of success or downfall. Throughout the leader's career, there was a steady stream or supply of advisors, financial backers, encouragers, kind strangers, and colleagues so that without such involvement, the leader's story may well have had a different outcome. What set the exemplary leaders apart in this area from the competent leaders was the nature of the advisors. Repeatedly the exemplary leaders cited a "moral voice," the "nudging moral elbow," or a "surrogate moral conscience" of some significant other guiding their thinking.

The "prodigious patrons" serve a substantive or monumental role in shaping and maintaining a leader's success and influence. The term "prodigious" is used because it means: monumental or consequential effect or outcome from a particular influence at a particular time. Prodigious also has the connotation of providence and fate, reflecting that timing of the influence was an essential factor in the eventual outcome. The prodigious people played such a role that, one is left to wonder, if that person had not acted when he or she did in the manner he or she did, the outcome of the specific sequence of events would have been significantly altered.

A "patron" is someone who does something on behalf of another and, hence, is a supporter of the person. The range of supporting activity is from a simple form of encouragement or advice to financial backing. At various points on each of the leaders time lines, patrons, whether a mother, father, sibling, spouse, peer, colleague, mentor, acquaintance, or stranger, prevented each leader from quitting, taking a different career path or missing fortuitous junctures in their rise to positions of prominent influence. Under the category of prodigious patron, the many examples that other's played in the careers of the leaders are numerous, critical and strategic.

Granted another source of encouragement, sound counsel, or financial provision may have risen up in a timely fashion, but there may not have been or the timing may not have been strategic for the leader. It could easily be argued that the leaders made the opportunities happen, and if the prodigious ones had not availed themselves, the nature of a leader would have found another source or made due. The biographies and autobiographies recognize that may be the case some of the time, but at other times the rhetoric used is "strategic turning point," "without whom, "influential" and "fortunate."

As already discussed, our leaders were fortunate to have their first prodigious patron be a parent or two. In their education, most people talked about benefiting from the affections of their teachers. Taking up the baton, others would follow to play prodigious roles in our leaders emerging and staying on the top. Welch (2001) captures this principle when he states, "Nearly everything I've done in my life has been accomplished with other people" (p. ix). In his prologue, Welch goes on to say about his story,

> Mostly, though, this is a story of what others have done – thousands of smart, self-confident, and energized employees who taught each other how to break the molds . . . . Their efforts and their success are what made my journey so rewarding. (p. xvi)

Welch prospers in his undergraduate studies, in part due to the mentoring and involvement of his faculty. Welch had faculty that took a special interest in him, devoting some extra time toward him, especially in his graduate studies. On one occasion, as a new graduate student, Welch got himself in trouble in his youthful folly. One professor came to his aide for leniency so that his potential could be developed in the graduate program.

While at graduate school, Welch met his first wife, who would be a source of support and encouragement, frequently instilling courage to do what is right when the demands as a CEO became particularly burdensome. He credits the support of his wife getting him through the most difficult day of his life, the day his mother died. His first wife was a devout catholic who continued his mother's religious influence in Welch's life.

Welch had an immediate supervisor his first year at General Electric (GE) who took notice of him. When Welch, feeling constrained by the bureaucracy of a large corporation, was quitting after his first year, Gutoff (one of Welch's superiors) spent four hours talking Welch into staying at GE with hopes of future opportunities for creativity, achievements and a differentiated reward system based on performance. Welch (2001) writes of one particular mentor named Herman Weiss, the vice chairman, and then comments generically:

> First a boss, then an ally and friend, Herm took me under his wing. It seemed everywhere I went I found a mentor. I wasn't searching for a surrogate father, but good people always seemed to crop up and give me their support. (p. 50)

Herm Weiss would continue to play a critical role for Welch's advancement to CEO. Welch (2002) reports Weiss's in the final days of struggle with cancer, "told Reg [Welch's predecessor] to keep his eye on me because I was "the person going places" (p. 64). Prior to that, Welch was not on Reg Jones' original list as a potential successor. Needing some specific experiences to be competitive and a well-rounded CEO, in his grooming, another colleague "helped me [Welch] find two people who would play critical roles in my career" (Welch, 2001, p. 67). Later in his career, Welch attributes his success to, more than ever, realizing "how much my success would depend on the people I hired. From my first day in plastics, I understood the importance of getting the right people" (p. 53). During the recession of the early 1980's, Welch attributes his success at this point of his tenure at GE to the fact that "we were fortunate. Our predecessors left a good balance sheet" (Welch, 2001, p. 126).

Walton attributes much of his success to being blessed with partners and 400,000 associates. In his autobiography, Walton (1992) states to his partners and associates, "This book is really your story" (p. vii). Similar to Welch, Walton (1992) reports, "All along, the history of Wal-Mart has been marked by having the right people in the right job when we needed them most" (p. 197).

Walton benefited greatly from the influence of his wife and her family. His wife Helen was very religious and even attended a Christian College for two years. When Walton wanted to open his first store in St. Louis as a partner with his buddy, it was Helen who insisted upon no partnership and wanted to relocate to a town with a population of 10,000 or less. Helen wanted small town values to permeate their family. It was Helen's "sharp elbow" and voice behind the establishment of the Wal-Mart Foundation and other altruistic ventures of the Walton Corporation.

Helen's parents were successful and happy. This was an inspiration and model of how to be a successful businessman and family man for Walton. Walton's father-in-law provided critical financial backing in the purchase of Walton's first store. Five years later, Walton's father-in-law would play an instrumental role in negotiating for Walton's new store.

Powell sees his life as "a story about the people who helped make me what I am. It is a story of my benefiting from opportunities created by the sacrifice of those who went before me and may be benefiting those who will follow" (Powell, 1995, p. viii).

After his parents and extended family, other people would take over in encouraging Powell. One unlikely source comes upon Powell's arrival to CCNY on the first day of classes. Powell (1995) shares:

> I felt overwhelmed. And then I heard a friendly voice: Hey, kid, you new? He was a short, red-faced, weather-beaten man with gnarled hands, and he stood behind a steaming cart of those giant pretzels that New Yorkers are addicted to. I had met a CCNY fixture called, for some unaccountable reason, "Raymond the Bagel Man," though he sold pretzels. I bought a warm, salty pretzel from Raymond, and we shot the breeze for a few minutes. That broke the ice for me. CCNY was some-how less intimidating. I was to become a regular of Raymond's over the next four and a half years. And it either speaks well of his character or poorly of my scholarship that while my memory of most of my professors have faded, the memory of Raymond the Bagel man remains undimmed. (p. 25)

It is interesting to note that Raymond the Bagel Man gets a paragraph devoted to him in Powell's autobiography. While the reason is not explicitly stated, it appears an emotional connection was established that, while initially breaking the ice of an intimidating experience, served other purposes such as having some one to share with on a personal level.

With a new infatuation directed toward a military society, Powell found a role model and club to provide a sense of belonging. Powell (1995) writes:

> One Pershing Rifles member impressed me from the start. Ronald Brooks was a young black man, tall, trim, handsome, the son of a Harlem Baptist Preacher and possessed maturity beyond most college students. Ronnie was only two years older than I, but something in him commanded deference. . . . Ronnie was sharp, quick, disciplined,

organized, qualities then invisible in Colin Powell. I had found a model and a mentor. I set out to remake myself in the Ronnie Brooks mold.

My experience in high school, on basketball and track teams, and briefly in Boy Scouting had never produced a sense of belonging or many permanent friendships. The Pershing Rifles did. For the first time in my life I was a member of a brotherhood. (p. 27, 28)

The relationship with Ronnie Brooks remained strong as years later on different paths, Ronnie was Powell's best man at his wedding. Early in his marriage, departing for his first Vietnam tour, Powell (1995) realized "that she [his wife] was going to make the perfect life partner for this soldier" (p. 76). She remained loyal and a constant support and anchor, providing Powell with the stability of a family in the context of a mobile military life. That their lives were viewed as a partnership toward bigger things prevented Powell from divided loyalties among his varied commitments and passions as a husband, father and military officer.

Powell was assigned to an unaccompanied tour to Korea. An unaccompanied tour meant leaving his wife for one year to raise their three children alone. His wife agreed it would be a hard sacrifice on her part, but stated, "if this is what you want, if this is what you think is best for you, then do it. Her support made it easier, but not easy" (p. 178). Celebrating their 30th wedding anniversary, Powell (1995) writes, "When the guests were gone, Alma and I sat amid the festive debris knowing we were richly blessed. And in the lottery of love and marriage, I knew that I had been the big winner" (p. 557).

Tracing his career, Powell cites the influence of various mentors and lessons learned that served him well as Chairman of the Joint Chief's of Staff. When his White House fellowship ended he states:

The people I had met during that year were going to shape my future in ways unimaginable to me then. But first I was off to Korea, where an old soldier would teach me a unique brand of military leadership. (Powell, 1995, p. 178)

His new leader in Korea would be a source of inspiration for Powell. The men he was leaving behind from his White House Fellowship were Casper Weinberger and Frank Carlucci who would later hold the highest Defense positions in Reagan's administration. Powell's contact and impressive work abilities with these men would facilitate his rise to the top when the time came.

The role others play in a leader's development is reflected in the following comments made by Powell (1995):

Had it not been for Tom Miller and Red Barrett in Germany, a Bill Abernathy and Cider Joe Stilwell at Fort Devens, a Charles Gettys in Vietnam, a Gunfighter Emerson in Korea, I would have left the Army

> long ago. These men gave our lives flavor, a spice, a texture, a mood,
> an atmosphere, an unforgetableness. (p. 203)

On several occasions, during some fleeting moments of foolishness in the early part of his career, Powell comments that his commanding officers, responding to his potential versus isolated incidents, proved valuable. One of the last evenings of his tour in Korea, in the context of a farewell party, a fight between men from two companies broke out in which Powell found himself involved. Powell states that if his commanding officer had been a lesser man and in today's Army, "such improper behavior . . . would likely have resulted in disciplinary action and ruined careers, including my own" (Powell, 1995, p. 200).

As a child, Marshall found a mentor with whom he was able to take frequent walks and find some solace. Stoler (1989) writes:

> Ashamed and humiliated by his academic performance and the
> treatment he received from his peers, distant from his father and his
> siblings, young Marshall responded by seeking approval and
> companionship elsewhere. John R. Wightman, a new, young pastor at
> his church . . . became a close friend and a major influence. (p. 6)

It appears having someone with whom to build a friendship was an important and timely influence. Graduating from VMI, Marshall was able to redeem himself somewhat with his father. Graduating as the Congress authorized the expansion of the army, mobilized Marshall, Sr. to help.

Marshall's father swung behind his son and organized a campaign to obtain the commission. Such a campaign was necessary because Marshall would need a letter of authorization from the War Department simply to take the examination, and such a letter required political connections. Marshall, Sr., sent a constant stream of inquiries and appeals to influential friends in Washington. Marshall Sr. made sure such recommendations went to the president and used every connection he had. As a result, the Pennsylvania senators made Marshall one of their allotted twenty-three nominees for the examination, noting, in a compliment to his father's methods as well as his own achievements, that he was "a young man of excellent connections and marked ability." (Stoler 1989, p 13)

A life long influence and boost to Marshall's career was being in the company of General Pershing. Of their relationship, Stoler (1989) documents that "he [Pershing] clearly did become Marshall's mentor, protector, supporter, and booster, and a powerful and influential one at that" (Stoler, 1989, p. 44). In 1924 Marshall would report, "No words can express the regret and loss I feel at the termination of my service with you. Few ever in life have such opportunities and almost none, I believe, such a delightful association as was mine with you" (Stoler, 1989, p. 44). They were to remain strong professional and personal friends until Pershing's death in 1948.

In 1927, Marshall becomes a deeply grieved widower. "Lily had been the center of his life and virtually his only emotional release" (Stoler, 1989, p. 54) to an otherwise private person. In 1930 Marshall would be fortunate to remarry:

> Katherine Marshall clearly provided her new husband with the emotional stability and outlet a man of his temperament needed. She also provided him with a ready-made family; three teenage children from her first marriage. Previously childless, Marshall now achieved additional emotional fulfillment as a stepfather, a role into which he fit easily and comfortably. Molly, the eldest, became his riding companion and close friend; Clifton and especially Allen, the youngest, were the sons he never had. (Stoler, 1989, p. 58)

During World War II, Marshall was able to effectively serve as the Chairman of the Joint Chief's of Staff because he could delegate responsibilities to competent people like Eisenhower, Bradley and Patton. While serving as secretary of state, Marshall had a stream of confidants and talent available.

Roosevelt credited Peabody as one the major influences of his life. Peabody was a man of high standards who appropriately challenged and inspired Roosevelt. Roosevelt found a hero in his cousin Theodore Roosevelt, not only taking advantage of the name, but of his example. Roosevelt was excited to follow in similar steps as Theodore Roosevelt (i.e., Harvard, Columbia, state assembly, Assistant Secretary of the Navy and governor of New York).

Roosevelt benefited greatly with his association with Louis McHenry Howe and his political prowess. Without the work of Howe (Roosevelt's advisor for most of his political life) and Eleanor Roosevelt, Franklin Roosevelt would probably have not been reelected to the state senate. Freidel (1990) recounts the details:

> The illness [typhoid fever] made the odds against Roosevelt's reelection to the state senate seem insurmountable. At this point a remarkable figure came to Roosevelt's rescue and became thenceforth his alter ego. This was Louis McHenry Howe, a resourceful, cynical newspaperman . . . . Further, Howe was a firm believer in the role of the great man in history. When Roosevelt, bedridden for the duration of the campaign, turned to him, Howe responded with enthusiasm, attaching his aspirations to the future of the handsome, charming young man. (p. 22)

Howe eventually served as Roosevelt's chief of staff. Between 1921, after FDR's diagnosis with polio, to 1928, winning the election to become the governor of New York is attributed in part to Howe, who, with Eleanor Roosevelt, kept Franklin prominent in politics, despite his 7-year respite and recuperation. Another friend would play a critical role in Roosevelt's sequences of successions. The Democratic Convention came close to not nominating

Roosevelt as their presidential candidate for the 1932 election. Much politicking and lobbying was required and an individual by the name of Garner made it happen. Freidel (1990) writes, "Garner played the decisive role in guaranteeing the nomination to Roosevelt" (p. 72).

Eleanor Roosevelt was strong-willed, forthright and a great political partner. Freidel (1990) states that "whatever the deficiencies in their intimate relationships, they became the greatest husband-and-wife political partners in American history" (p. 36). She would be Roosevelt's moral conscience, part of his kitchen cabinet, and would continuously place books in front of Roosevelt for him to read. Freidel observes:

> Eleanor Roosevelt herself, with her own entourage, served much of the times, as she had in New York State, as her husband's eyes and ears. She was also his conscience, prodding him on social justice matters such as the need to help black people in their plight. She had much influence on him, and also developed into something of an independent political force of her own right. (p. 123)

As Roosevelt grew in stature, he attracted and surrounded himself with excellent people. Burns (1984) states:

> Outside his family and personal staff were a host of advisers, political associates and correspondents. These men provided something of a measure of the President-elect's ideas and purposes. Two things were remarkable about the men around Roosevelt in 1932: the variety of their backgrounds and ideas, and the fact that not one of them dominated the channels of access to Roosevelt's mind. It was a varied group because Roosevelt's test of a man was not his basic philosophy, or lack of one, but the sweep of his information, his ability to communicate, and his willingness to share ideas. Without any plan, a "brain trust," as the reporters came to call it, grew up around him. (p. 153)

Gandhi benefited greatly from the advice of a family friend. Because times had changed from when his father began his career, he believed Gandhi would fare better pursuing studies to become a barrister-at-law in England. Such a title would be easier to obtain and take less time than to qualify as a lawyer in India. Not doing well in college and not necessarily liking studies, yet recognizing the title would afford more opportunities, the advice resonated in Gandhi's thinking. The question was how to afford it. To make it work would require a financial sponsor. His brother and extended family came to his aid, with his brother seeing financial sponsorship of Gandhi as an investment in the future.

Gandhi's transition in England was much aided by Dr. Mehta, a friend of the family. Dr. Mehta provided arrangements for adequate housing, an apprenticeship for Gandhi to have an adequate experience in England and frequent advice. Gandhi's various landlords would take an interest in him and help him adjust to the culture of England while at same time strengthening his ties to his Indian heritage.

The kindness of a stranger made it possible for Gandhi to arrive in South Africa in a timely fashion. On the day he was to sail, due to an error, no cabins were available for Gandhi. The chief officer, hearing of Gandhi's plight availed an extra berth in his cabin to Gandhi. This act of kindness prevented Gandhi from being stranded in Bombay for one month and missing his rendezvous with the chain of events to be set in motion in South Africa.

On a trip to India, Gandhi raised the public awareness of the Indian cause in South Africa. The Europeans in South Africa heard about Gandhi's stirring of the public in India. As a result, upon returning to South Africa, Gandhi was accosted by a mob that almost killed him. The amazing act of bravery by a stranger spared Gandhi from potentially losing his life. Chadha (1992) records the incident with vivid detail:

> The crowd was cursing and shouting, and Gandhi was in danger of his life. Stones, brickbats, mud and rotten fish were being hurled at him. Someone dislodged his turban; someone else struck him with a riding whip. A burly fellow came up to the Mahatma-to-be, slapped him in the face and then kicked him hard. He was gripping the railing of a house nearly unconscious. 'I had almost given up the hope of reaching home alive,' he wrote. . . . At that moment Mrs. Alexander the wife of the police superintendent saw what was happening. She advanced into the fray with an open umbrella to keep off the flying missiles and stood between the crowd and Gandhi, protecting him at least against hard blows until the constables arrived to accompany him to the house where his family was waiting. (p. 80)

As Gandhi became more active in Indian affairs, both in India and South Africa, he networked with influential people. One in particular was the scholar Gokhale, who with his contacts and ideology was much an ally to Gandhi. Chadha (1997) states of their relationship:

> With the death of Gokhale there was a deep void in Gandhi's life. "Launching on the stormy sea of Indian public life, I was in need of a sure pilot," he wrote years later. "I had one in Gokhale and had felt secure in his keeping. Now that he was gone, I was thrown on my own resources." (p. 207)

Similar narratives exist for the competent leaders, people ranging from strangers to friends, colleagues, mentors, followers, and spouses served prodigious roles in the emergence of the leaders. Gates had Paul Allen, two years Gates' senior, who since their days together at Lakeside Academy, to starting Micro-Soft together, was a synergistic compliment to Gates. Ford had

Couzens, Wills and Malcomson as business partners and colleagues who provided a strategic and essential compliment to their leader. Ford also had Edison, first as an inspiration, then as a colleague and, eventually, a close friend.

The one noticeable contrast between the exemplary leaders' circle of prodigious patrons and the competent leaders' patrons was the prevalence of a moral voice or conscience influencing their thinking and actions. Roosevelt, while active in church, had Eleanor who was very much his conscious with attention and passion for social issues. Gandhi had his religious teachings very much guiding his philosophies. Welch had a very religious mother and attended the Catholic Church until her death. Also, Welch's first wife was a devout catholic. Being a good catholic and a good businessman was important and doable in Welch's mind. Walton, while a churchgoer, had a devoutly religious wife who kept his moral compass pointing in the general direction of north. Powell made it a point to remain involved in his church throughout his various tours of duty. Marshall's childhood mentor was a young pastor.

Hitler and Mao were swept away in their Marxist, Lenin and socialist ideologies, the end very much justified the means, atrocious or not. With Patton and MacArthur, they were pretty much the center of their world, and while war heroes, it appears war was their stage. Both had a spouse and a parent who instilled the belief they were of great stock and, hence, they were to be great. Gates was so immersed in his business that, prior to his recent marriage, there was not much recorded outside influence.

Ford is the one anomaly in this case study. Ford's wife was very much a believer in Ford during the entrepreneurial stage of his business. She sacrificed personal comfort and financial security when frugality was demanded and risks taken. She never complained and worked around Ford's obsessive-compulsive drive in building an automobile. She was his greatest supporter. As a regular churchgoer, Nevins (1954) writes:

> Clara Bryant Ford, credited by her husband with 'foresighted policy,' read letters from Ford employees and their wives , and may have been helpful in molding Henry Ford's attitudes in humanitarian matters. A New York sculptor to who Ford sat at this very time, C. S. Pietro, reports him as speaking of her in the warmest terms: "she instilled into his mind he [Ford] said, those ideals of social justice which he is trying to make practical, and has kept his heart young and fresh and has enabled him to maintain his faith in God and man." (p. 540)

After some public set backs, Ford's autocratic tendencies heightened and his insecurities grew which made him vulnerable to the corrupting and self-serving counsel of Bennett, his emerging confidant beginning around 1919. In a parasitic relationship, Bennett gained Ford's confidence and was able to filter information that tickled Ford's ears and forced distance between Ford and Edsel and other Ford executives. If Ford, while having some idiosyncratic tendencies toward autocracy, would have died earlier in his life, pre 1915, he may well have been considered an exemplary leader given the initiatives of his company, the improvement of the welfare of his workers, and his contributions to society at large.

Ford had proven himself a conscientious businessman and citizen in a variety of ways. He attempted to negotiate peace in Europe with his Peace Ship. He made the automobile affordable for the masses. He changed industry standards by improving the quality of work life with a $5 workday and an eight-hour shift. Also, Ford authorized a Sociological Department to improve the quality of life for his workers.

Prior to being tainted by his failed ventures in the public arena, Ford had a sense of moral obligation to his workers and the larger world. His failures resulted in large-scale public embarrassment, heightening his insecurities and pushing him to become all the more autocratic with his company. At the same time, there was a changing of the guard of Ford's confidants that successfully secluded Ford from moral and reasonable counsel and put an even greater distance between Ford and his son Edsel.

Suffice it to say, the most influential variable facilitating the emergence of the leaders of this study was the stream of prodigious patrons. Out of all the people and interactions in the leader's life, specific acts of kindness, whether in word or deed, would take on prodigious meaning in the emergence of the leader to the point of his influence. What appear to be required are prodigious patrons along the whole aspect of the leader's progression. It is not the same person at all times. Each new arena of performance appears to bring another set of prodigious patrons. The caliber of one's prodigious patrons is a determinative influence whether a leader emerges exemplary or not. Just as bad company corrupts good morals, good company reinforces good morals.

The important and necessary role patrons play in developing leaders is captured by Farson (1997) when he states:

> We forget sometimes that leadership is a shared role played partly by people who are not titular leaders. Kings have regents whispering in their ears. Presidents have advisers. CEOs have consultants. Managers have assistants who help shape their behavior but who do not take the risks of leadership and who do not get the credit. (p. 146)

Critics and Adversaries

Having a series of prodigious patrons is necessary for leaders to develop. One's opponents, adversaries and, in some cases, even enemies serve a determinative force in influencing the emergence of influential leaders. On the first level, competition raises the standard of performance for leaders to develop and display their best, pushing their limits to excel to be better than the competition. Opponents force the leaders to refine their positions, provide a context for defining moments, and allow for victories. Whether gracious or hostile, opponents serve a determining influence on the emerging leaders thinking and resolve for action.

Marshall's brother provided the goad that was the precursor to the average child distinguishing himself. Marshall's ambition to excel was initially fueled, Mosely (1982) states, by:

> . . . . a burning determination to put one over on his sneering, superior and hypercritical elder brother. For one day, after Stuart had heard his parents talking about sending George to VMI, he burst out with objections. What? Send that worthless shaver to his old college? Not if he could help it! He rushed to talk to his mother, and Marshall overheard them. "He was trying to persuade her not to let me go [to VMI]," Marshall said later, "because he thought I would disgrace the family name. Well, that made more impression on me than all the instructors, parental pressure, or anything else. I decided then and there that I was going to wipe his eye. (p. 10)

For Gandhi, discussions with atheists and various Christians was formative in Gandhi defining his religious convictions. When first arriving in South Africa Gandhi reported:

> I am a Hindu by birth but I do not know much about Hinduism. In fact I do not know where I am, and what is and what should be my belief. I intend to make a careful study of my own religion and, as far as I can, of other religions as well. (Chadha, 1997, p. 56)

His discussions with an atheist, zealous Christians and other Hindus would soon force him to solidify his beliefs. His religious beliefs would merge with his political beliefs. Witnessing the discrimination toward Indians in South Africa and experiencing some harsh racism, Gandhi was moved to lead the cause in promoting rights for Indians.

The more extreme example of adversaries having a determinative influence comes from Hitler. It was only as a soldier during WWI that Hitler developed any functional skills. Post-war Germany was ripe for radical groups and ideas in which Hitler could find a cause to identify with and serve. In addition, it appears the conditions of post WWI Germany were even conducive for Hitler to surface as a leader for the nation. Patton and MacArthur felt they needed the context of war to shine and gain fame, with Patton especially concerned that the end of the wars would come prematurely before he would have the opportunity to become a hero or a martyr. It is often with the background of enemies that heroes appear on the foreground.

Roosevelt benefited from the criticism of his articulate political opponents by changing his practices and policies at times. Rightly accused of not defining his position on certain key issues in his campaign for the presidency, "to avoid future disaster" (Freidel, 1990, p. 68), Roosevelt learned from his mistakes and opponents' comments. Roosevelt even enlisted advisers with diverse views to benefit his decisions by having a full analysis of the complex issues. Political opponents kept the important issues in the forefront, which helped define Roosevelt's position on the diverse issues facing the country.

Mao emerged a leader in the context of competing forces and ideologies in the cultural revolution taking place in China. The Long March only strengthened an already strong resolve and led to the eventual rise of the Chinese Communist Party (CCP).

The competition in the relatively new world of personal computers required Gates to work at a relentless pace. He worked 12-hour days so that his company could take the lead in the computer software business. As a result, innovative software and operating systems evolved. Manes and Andrews (1993) cite, "Microsoft has been the single greatest beneficiary of inept competition of any company in the world" (p. 245).

For Welch, friendly adversaries, whether on the golf course, hockey rink, or corporate world helped make the competitive edge a driving force. Walton respectfully acknowledges the role of his competitors in helping Wal-Mart become great. Ford's early backers became his critics in wanting Ford to bring his car to production earlier than Ford was ready for. The lawsuit by the Dodge Brothers against Ford forced him to share a larger portion of company dividends with stockholders versus reinvesting in the company. Losing the lawsuit became an impetus for Ford to gain sole control of the Ford Motor Company. By resigning as President, he could start his own company. With such a threat, Ford Motor Company stock became undervalued allowing him to buy out the stockholders. Ford soon became the sole owner and was unhindered in expansion and development of the Ford Motor Company.

Unfortunately, other adversaries had a detrimental effect on Ford. On June 22, 1916, the Chicago Tribune ran a story that was wrongly informed, portraying Ford as unpatriotic for not providing wages for employees on active guard duty. The next day an editorial called Ford an anarchist. When the paper failed to print a retraction, Ford filed a libel suit for one million dollars. The case unfortunately centered on proving "Ford was an ignorant idealist and an unpatriotic man" (Nevins, 1957, p. 131). In the trial, two and a half years later, Ford took the stand for cross-examination. Nevins (1957) poignantly describes the humiliation:

> . . . he was subjected to eight days of merciless inquisition by Elliott G. Stevenson. Setting verbal traps, and playing upon the manufacturer's ignorance in general fields of knowledge, Stevenson

essayed to prove that he was totally unqualified to serve as a guide in politico-social fields. . . . His very honesty played into Stevenson's hands, for where anybody with a little more of a serpent's guild would have been shrewdly evasive, he was naively frank. . . . As Stevenson probed deeper, Ford made an unhappy spectacle. He sat slightly slumped forward, cupping his chin in hand, his body turning from side to side, his feet twisting nervously. In the Dodge suit he had talked fluently and interestingly about familiar technical and corporate subjects. But at Mt. Clemens [neutral site for the trial], led into a bog of cultural knowledge and dictionary definitions, he floundered helplessly. (pp. 135, 136)

The embarrassing display of ignorance earned Ford smirks and chuckles from those present and continued as his ignorance was humiliatingly portrayed in the Tribunes coverage of the trial. Adding to Ford's shame was the outcome of the trial. While the jury found the Tribune guilty of libel, the award was only six cents. Nevins (1957) reports:

Unquestionably the rough buffets he took in these years, the Dodge suit verdict, the ridicule of the Peace Ship, the misrepresentation of the five-dollar day, the cheating and name-calling in the Newberry campaign, the slaying of the League, the Tribune trial—blunted the edge of the fine idealism so marked in him before the World War. . . . Thus the trial, which did not break the closed system of his thought or persuade him to seek a broader cultivation, tinged his mind with wariness, bitterness, and cynicism. (p. 141, 142)

Nevins (1957) goes on to add:

The scars, which the Tribune suit left upon Henry Ford, were thus a public misfortune. It was a greater public misfortune that his quest in these years for an occupation outside his company, which would satisfy his altruistic impulses, did not open some modestly suitable field and give him some really helpful associates. He was thrown back upon himself." (p. 142)

Faithful are the wounds of a friend since those who wound us at times can be doing a friendly service. As iron sharpens iron, so do our opponents keep our leaders sharp, but as evident with Ford and in the case of war, too much iron or sharpening can be devastating.

Apprenticeships/Sequences of Success

Not only did people play a strategic role in accelerating the leaders to arenas of influence, certain events played critical roles in maturing and showcasing natural and developed competencies. With each success, the emerging leaders gradually gained experience, confidence and recognition of their abilities. This became a new starting point for the next sequence of events in the advancement of their careers. In addition, it is in the context of learning in success that new lessons emerged. Getting the attention of superiors and colleagues solicited additional opportunities. Welch (2001) says it well of one particular transition point, "this new job put me on the radar screen" (p. 49). After his first tour of duty in Germany, Powell (1995) comments, "I bid a sentimental goodbye to the 48th Infantry. I had joined as a rookie, and I was leaving as a fairly seasoned pro" (p. 54).

As Mao got more involved in the revolutionary activities and the formation of the Communist Party of China, his ability to organize the laborers and write and debate persuasively got him noticed. Mao soon emerged as an acknowledged leader, eventually rising to a member of the national team. Mao continued to publish, speak and organize, continually developing his abilities and even drawing the attention of Stalin.

After a series of set backs in the growth of the Red Army and the CCP, Mao's only recourse was what evolved into the Long March. Approximately 86,000 people marched a 6,000-mile long retreat that took over one year. Other communists joined the march to avoid the opposing armies and in hopes to keep the CCP alive and secure a new stronghold for the CCP to operate. The Long March became a fateful and symbolic victory for the CCP even though, between the battles, disease and starvation, only 10% of the original troops arrived. While the Long March was a retreat, "it had put him [Mao] on the brink of being China's most promising political leader" (Terrill, 1999, p. 165).

Previously living in a house for the destitute poor, squandering his inheritance and outgrowing his orphan's pension, Hitler's very first success was in the battlefield as a volunteer in the Bavarian regiment. Despite being initially found unfit for military service in the Austrian army and luckily avoiding a prison sentence for dodging the draft, he held his first long-term job as a volunteer in the army. Hitler served as a dispatch runner for four years. While he earned some medals, he was never promoted beyond the rank of private, first class. "Hitler led a charmed life during the war, and he seems to have been obscurely aware that he was one of the fortunate ones who would never be seriously wounded" (Payne, 1973, p. 109).

After the armistice, Hitler was selected to be a political speaker. Fest (1992) reports:

> . . . for an enlightenment squad attached to the Lechfeld camp for returning soldiers. The squad was there to exert influence on the men, indoctrinating them with nationalistic, anti-Marxist ideas. In addition, the assignment was meant as a practical course in speaking and agitation for the squad members. In the barrack of Camp Lechfeld, Hitler developed his gift for oratory and practical psychology. (p. 114)

In classes preparing Hitler for his duties, he was singled out by his commanding officers as a natural orator. Gaining a reputation, Hitler was soon given the responsibility of investigating different radical parties that had resurfaced after Germany's defeat. One particular assignment led to Hitler finding a permanent home. When the discussion moved to separating Bavaria from Prussia, Hitler could not but speak. Outshining the previous speaker, he drew the attention of the leaders of the small German Workers Party. Eventually, recruited as a member, Hitler's speaking abilities brought a significant increase of people to the political rallies and party membership. Hitler's "growing reputation as a speaker solidified his position inside the party" (Fest, 1992, p. 121). He soon left the army for full time service in the leadership of the National Socialist German Workers Party. As the growing party's most visible figure, he rose to the rank of director of propaganda, now part of the leadership's inner circle.

Upon his return from England, Gandhi was unable to make a go of it in establishing his career practicing law. He was even denied a teaching position because he was not a university graduate. Then he got a break. A shipping company with interests in India and South Africa was involved in a litigation case. The European lawyers were in need of someone to provide counsel from an Indian perspective. His success in a tertiary role helped him establish influential contacts that became the launching pad for representing Indian rights in South Africa. After a series of small victories, he established a reputation as an effective mobolizer and guardian of oppressed Indians.

Roosevelt, having secured a New York state senate seat, in part by name, "gained attention throughout the state and even beyond its border" (Freidel, 1990, p. 19). Campaigning for Wilson allowed Roosevelt to impress party elder Mr. Daniels, who became the Secretary of the Navy in Wilson's cabinet. Roosevelt earned an appointment as Assistant Secretary of the Navy, in which his seven years of service managed "greatly to advance his political education and his standing as a promising Democratic figure" (Freidel, 1990, p. 23).

Although quite active in politics up to 1921, when he was first diagnosed with polio, Roosevelt would not hold another public office until seven years later when fortuitous timing allowed him to win the election for New York Governor by a victory by 25,000 votes. As governor, Roosevelt went to the radio. "He [Roosevelt] developed to perfection a simple, conversational way of talking, in happy contrast to conventional political oratory. When he became president, he continued these talks as the 'Fireside Chats'" (Freidel, 1990, p. 58). The Fireside Chats and his warm style of relating endeared Roosevelt to the nation, aiding him to win three reelections.

Between 1879 and 1882, Ford worked at the Michigan Car Company, Flower's Machine Shop and the Detroit Dry Dock. These jobs were all self-imposed transitions for him to gain experience with machines. His various apprenticeships prepared him to take a position servicing steam engines in 1882 with Westinghouse. During this period of work, much of his leisure time was spent experimenting with machines and engines. In 1891, he relocated his family from stable and secure roots to work as a technician in Edison's Illuminating Company. With his developed propensity for mechanics and competence as an engineer, Ford was soon promoted to chief engineer. With the additional pay and discretionary time, Ford was able to make all the more progress on his creation of the horseless carriage. Ford, with success in developing a horseless carriage attracted backers. Winning an automobile race provided additional notoriety, confidence and financial backers. "As his reputation increased, Ford had made distinguished friends who helped broaden his experience and increase his interest in the world beyond the factory" (Nevins, 1957, p.20).

Walton seemed to live a charmed life with success as Missouri's youngest Eagle Scout until that time, quarterbacking for the high school state football champions and as a senior guard for the high school's state basketball champions. Such experiences "taught me to expect to win, to go into tough challenges always planning to come out victorious . . . Thinking like that often seems to turn into sort of a self-fulfilling prophecy" (Walton, 1992, p.18). Logically, Walton's early success as a retailer resulted in acquiring additional stores and eventually leading to exponential growth of the Wal-Mart chain.

Powell, finding his niche and a focus for his youth in the ROTC, soon distinguished himself. In his junior year, Powell became the ROTC's pledge officer and obtained the highest number of pledges. Powell (1995) reports that it was a defining moment in his life as it was "the first small indication that I might be able to influence the outcome of events" (p. 32).

Upon his return from summer ROTC training at Fort Bragg, Powell was distinguished as "Best Cadet, Company D." Powell (1995) writes, "the summer of 1957 was a triumph for me . . . I was bringing my parents something they had never had from me – proof, with my desk set, that I had at last excelled" (p. 35). Because Powell was a "Distinguished Military Graduate" he "was offered a regular rather than a reserve commission, which meant that I would have to serve three rather than two years on active duty. I eagerly accepted" (Powell, 1995 p. 37).

Following basic school, Powell requested and received orders to attend both the Ranger and Airborne schools. Because of his distinguished career, in 1965, Powell was tapped for the Infantry Officers Advanced Course, finishing first among a class of 200. Soon after, he was assigned as instructor of the school. Years later Powell would reflect that going to instructors' school was extremely helpful in preparing him for his role in front of cameras and speaking to large audiences. In 1967, Powell was assigned to the Army Command and General Staff College at Fort Leavenworth, Kansas where he graduated second among the army's pool of elite officers. Powell returned to the front-line in Vietnam, and as a result of a timely photo and story in the *Army Times,* his career took a significant change. Overnight he "went from looking after eight hundred men to planning warfare for nearly eighteen thousand troops, artillery units, aviation battalions and a fleet of 450 helicopters" (Powell, 1995, p. 135). Roth (1993) relates the story:

> One day the Americal Division commander was reading his copy of the weekly newspaper *Army Times* when he saw a story about the most recent Command and General Staff College graduating class. There before him on the page was a picture of one of his officers, the number-two man in the class, Major Powell. The division commander, Major General Charles Gettys, is reported to have exclaimed, "I've got the number-two Leavenworth graduate in my division and he's stuck out in the boonies. I want him on my staff! (p. 83)

Once Marshall's military brilliance was on the radar screen, he rose as an aide to high-ranking generals which "continued to offer Marshall distinct opportunities otherwise unavailable no matter how rapid his advancement might have been" (Stoler, 1989, p. 42). Eventually, his competence and character would lead him to being requested to serve as an aide to General Pershing. While Pershing was the "General of the Army" and would become the army's chief of staff in 1921; as Pershing's aide, Marshall would be "introduced to the highest level of military and political leadership and would receive an education in politico-military affairs unavailable in another position" (Stoler, 1989, p. 42). "Still under forty, Marshall had emerged to General Pershing's chief tactical advisers and most extraordinary officers. . . He also developed an unexcelled competence and reputation for his diplomatic ability to arrange and operate within Allied commands" (Stoler, 1989, p. 41).

Welch's series of promotions in GE, based upon rewards for outstanding performance, put Jack "on the radar screen . . . becoming a real player" (Welch, 2001, p.49). Rigorous differentiation based on merit and performance in the context of supporting people became one of Welch's emphases as CEO of GE. Welch benefited and, hence, practiced getting and rewarding the right people.

As is already known, success breeds success and opportunity favors the prepared. In the case of our leaders, the platforms for initial success came from initial opportunities being available for the leaders to shine. Early successes played an important role in giving the emerging leaders a sense of control over their destinies as well as new competencies. Sample (2002) states a similar theme in his research on leadership, "And yet many of the world's greatest leaders demonstrated relatively little aptitude for leadership in their youth, but instead learned the esoteric art through study, apprenticeship and practice" (Sample, 2001, p. 2).

However, it is worthwhile to point out, in the context of an alarming number of successes, our leaders experienced their share of failures. Walton, after establishing a successful first and second store, had to start over again when the owner of the building refused to renew Walton's lease so he could have the store for his son. Walton's lack of foresight in negotiating for a long-term lease or purchasing the building for his store would be a mistake he would make only once. Welch fortuitously did not get the ROTC scholarship. While only with GE for three years, Welch recounts, "I had actually blown up a factory – for real!. . . . As the boss, I was clearly at fault" (Welch, 2001, p. 27, 28). Welch's superiors' responses modeled that experimenting is acceptable and to learn from one's mistakes was part of maturing.

Roosevelt was deeply disappointed that he did not get tapped, like his role model Teddy Roosevelt, for the Porcelian, a club at the top of the hierarchy at Harvard. "Eleanor Roosevelt thought the disappointment impelled him to be more democratic" (Freidel, 1990, p. 11). Roosevelt failed some classes at Columbia law school. Gandhi dropped out of college after his first term and, upon his return from England, was not able to establish his own law practice in India. Early in his military career, Powell received a soft reprimand for losing his sidearm. In today's army such a *faux pas* would have significant implications for a young officer's career. His commanding officer's "example of humane leadership that does not always go by the book was not lost on me. When they fall down, pick 'em up, dust 'em off, pat 'em on the back, and move 'em on" (Powell, 1995, p. 46). Another time, Powell lost the train tickets for his platoon in route to Munich and, as a result, was stranded in the Frankfurt Bahnhof. Powell (1995) says it well, "nobody ever made it to the top by never getting into trouble" (p. 47).

Gates and Ford, through persistent trial and error in the development of their products, ultimately became the victors, but it consisted of failures and setbacks of their own. Regarding Ford, Nevin's (1957) states:

> Ford's saddest creative failure lay in his relationship with his son, to whom he gave intense devotion and total incomprehension. Edsel was a man of the finest qualities, upright, idealistic, public-spirited, and highly intelligent. The father's mistaken belief that he lacked toughness and drive led to sadism and tragedy. "He tried to remake Edsel in his own image," says Sorenson – and whether this is true or not, he certainly acted with a tragic lack of insight or sympathy. (p. 619, 620)

All emerging leaders will do well to take comfort in the fact that success and failure are often the different sides to the same coin. Our emerging leaders of influence had superiors or prodigious patrons around them who could normalize failures as part of the development equation.

Educators and society will do well to provide many opportunities for students to demonstrate and display success. David of the Bible was able to conquer Goliath after developing competence in similar situations of slaying lions and bears with his sling. While it is often considered getting a big break that opens up a person's career, it appears there are a series of small breaks, part timing and part merit based, that create or promote additional opportunities for influence. The above examples illustrate the importance of a series of minor victories via mini-apprenticeships that open the door for bigger victories. The examples cited are but just a few of those types of experiences permeating the life of each leader in their rise in influence.

Favorable Fate

Our leaders emerged to a position of influence both by accident and design. While the leaders were very much active agents in their destiny, their destiny took on bigger proportions and directions beyond what was initially imagined. Opportunities provided choices for the leaders and choices provided the leaders opportunities. There were times when fate seemed to be more determinative than it often gets credit for. The timing of some circumstances provided the same sense of fortuitous advantage that some of the prodigious patrons afforded the leaders. Mao frequently had his life spared. Early in the organization of the revolution, opposing forces brutally quenched the revolutionary forces. "Thirty thousand people were slaughtered in Hunan that summer. Mao was lucky not to have been one of them" (Terrill, 1999, p. 114). Mao was eventually captured and marched to a compound to be shot. After a desperate dash in the spray of bullets he was able to hide in the grass.

> Mao crouched in silence and devout hope. A couple of times the soldiers came so close that he could have reached out and touched them. Half a dozen times he gave up hope and felt certain they had seen him. Dusk bailed him out. The troops ended the search and went off for dinner. (Terrill, 1999, p. 117)

Mao was part of the original 10% who survived the Long March, a 6000-mile long retreat. Mao, Terrill (1999) states:

> . . . enjoyed a good deal of luck. His own body escaped the knife by a hair's breadth three or four times. He gained control of the CCP at the end of the Long March in part because his archrival had bad luck while struggling through Tibet. (p. 460)

MacArthur had many close calls with death. On his retreat from the Philippines on a PT boat, it was speculated his chances of getting through the Japanese blockade were 1 in 5. After some close encounters in which they had to kill the engine to avoid being detected, the PT boat made it to Cagayan. Catching a flight that night to Australia, they missed, by 10 minutes, the

Japanese dive-bombers in pursuit of them. When MacArthur safely landed in Australia, he remarked to his aide, "It was close, but that's the way it is in war. You win or lose, live or die – and the difference is just an eyelash" (MacArthur, 1964, p. 145). On his first assignment in the Philippines, while on patrol, an ambusher's "bullet tore through the crown of his campaign hat and into a sapling behind him" (Manchester, 1978, p. 64). While on a reconnaissance mission in Mexico, a gun battle ensued.

> The horsemen put three bullet holes through MacArthur's clothes and wounded one of his Mexicans; he shot four of the assailants. Near Laguna, three more mounted men fired at him. Again lead tore MacArthur's uniform. (Manchester, 1978, p. 76)

Patton suffered various wounds with one, in particular, just missing an artery, sciatic nerve and all the vital parts. "His wound was miraculous, and he ascribed his good luck to fate" (Blumenson, 1985, p 115). Patton was hospitalized for three months with a life threatening blood clot following an injury from his horse. At least twice, Patton suffered head injuries from his riding, once receiving a direct kick in the head from his horse. He suffered injuries from a gasoline lamp blowing up in his face. While driving to Paris his "car ran into a railway gate and the jolt sent Patton's head through the windshield. He cut an artery on the temple" (Blumenson, 1985, p. 99). As a teenager, Patton was left unconscious following an automobile accident.

In Vietnam, Powell says that many times "he had come so close to being killed" in combat (Powell, 1995, p. 95). A branch spared Powell from a direct hit by mortar when others around him were wounded. Timing was an accelerant to his already advancing career. Following his graduation as second in his class from Leavenworth, the *Army Times* carried his picture and the story. The paper ended up in Powell's commander's hands in Vietnam, which, in turn, became the impetus for Powell's transfer to headquarters. Reagan took office and named Casper Weinberger and Frank Carlucci, who Powell had worked with eight-and-a-half years earlier, to his two top Defense Department posts. "When Powell was rejoined with those who first welcomed him to Washington, it may have been Providence of fate but it was not maneuvering" (Roth, 1993, p. 110). The established relationship Powell had with the new regime became strategic in his eventual rise to Chairman of the Joint Chief of Staffs.

For Hitler, chance continued to seem to intervene. Biographer Fest (1992) writes, "but again, as was to happen repeatedly, chance came to his aid" (p. 61). As a draft dodger, Hitler avoided a jail sentence because of the timing of the paperwork. Runners in the army usually got killed. Not Hitler, while wounded twice, he escaped death or serious injury, unlike so many of his fellow soldiers and runners. Hitler was randomly assigned to report on the activities of the German Workers Party. The chance meeting allowed for Hitler to meet Drexler who, in turn, recruited Hitler and provided the platform and opportunities for Hitler to begin his ascent to power. In any other era, Hitler would probably not have emerged a leader. Payne (1973) states:

> Hitler's rise to power could be measured mathematically by the rising curve of unemployment figures. Misery and destitution were his storm troopers. The more helplessly the Germans floundered in poverty the more they were attracted to that strange political agitator who promised that once he was in power all their troubles would be ended. (p. 233)

Payne (1973) goes on to document how "the times favored violence, intrigue, and desperate stratagems" (p. 237). Fest (1992) reports, "from the spring of 1943 on, there was a series of attempts at assassination. Not one came off, either because of technical failure, or Hitler's knack for scenting danger, or because some seemingly incredible chance intervened" (p. 700).

Marshall's entrance into the military following his graduation from VMI was, in part, the result of congress passing a bill for the expansion of the military with an increase of 837 first and second lieutenants. Marshall's graduation a year earlier or a year later may well have missed the window of opportunity presented by congress. With valor and distinction in a skirmish in the war, Marshall was promoted to the rank of temporary full colonel. Immediately upon his promotion, he was requested by Pershing to come to the General Staff of the American Expeditionary Force (AEF) at headquarters. The disappointing immediate transfer more than likely saved Marshall's life from a battle that "he almost certainly would not have survived" (Mosely, 1982, p. 64). Mosley (1984) records Marshall's writing on the incident:

> Hurriedly packing my few effects and saying goodbye to my friends, I prepared to start by automobile at six o' clock the next morning. . . . Six days later they dashed into the great counterattack, which precipitated the retreat of the German Army, and within seventy-two hours every field and all four of the lieutenant colonels were killed, and every battalion commander was a casualty, dead or wounded. (p. 64)

Roosevelt was ready to sneak away from Groton to go fight in the Spanish War. At that crucial time, scarlet fever intervened. More than likely, if in his youthful zeal he would have left to fight, he would have probably missed his rendezvous with his destiny. Documenting the complicated affairs throughout Roosevelt's presidency, Freidel (1990) writes, "at this point, chance again intervened" (p. 458), morbidly referencing the early demise of a potential political opponent, which saved Roosevelt a political embarrassment. On another occasion, Roosevelt narrowly missed assassination when a woman tugged on the arm of the assailant just ten yards away, ruining the aim of the five shots fired. In terms of entering politics, Burns (1984) states, "Roosevelt did not create his first great opportunity. That opportunity came to him" (p. 29). A friend visiting Roosevelt on a legal errand shared that a state assembly seat may open up and asked if Roosevelt would be interested in running. "Once Roosevelt made up his mind, the party leaders managed things easily" (Burns, 1984, p. 30). Roosevelt's political education began.

Burns (1984) is even more explicit in the role of luck when he states:

> Climbing the political ladder to the presidency, according to one theory, is essentially a matter of luck; the winner has simply won an incredible throw of the dice. This theory can be easily applied to Roosevelt; his wealth, name, family connections, appearance were bestowed upon him, and he had the good luck to run for office during two Democratic years. Yet he had bad luck too. In 1912, in the middle of his campaign for re-election to the state senate, he was stricken by typhoid fever and put out of action for the rest of the contest. (p. 44)

Burns (1984) goes on to describe the good fortune of having Howe as campaign manager, who was able to secure a victory for Roosevelt despite Roosevelt's inability to campaign.

Gandhi had a brief period in which spending idle time with certain peers was having a corruptive influence on him. When his friend took him to a brothel, he was spared only by God who Gandhi states, "in His infinite mercy protected me against myself" (Gandhi, 1948, p. 37). Gandhi saw fate much at work in his life. Gandhi (1948) writes:

> There are some actions from which an escape is a godsend both for the man who escapes and for those about him. Man, as soon as he gets back his consciousness of right, is thankful to the Divine mercy for the escape. As we know that a man often succumbs to temptation, however much he may resist it, we also know that Providence often intercedes and saves him in spite of himself. How all this happens, -- how far a man is free and how far a creature of circumstance, -- how far free will comes into play and where fate enters on the scene, -- all this is a mystery and will remain a mystery. (p. 37)

The same day of Gandhi's farewell party back to India after a year in South Africa, Gandhi came across a story in the local newspaper describing the Franchise Amendment Bill. At the farewell party, Gandhi "warned his compatriots: 'it is the first nail in our coffin. It strikes at the root of our self-respect'" (Chadha, 1977, p. 64). Gandhi's friends convinced Gandhi to stay and fight for Indian rights in South Africa. The timing of the reading of the story and the forum of the farewell party of allowing for discussion on the matter converged so that Gandhi's career as a liberator for Indian rights began.

Walton, as a pilot, flew frequently to his stores, once he had to make an emergency landing due to engine failure. Welch believes it was a blessing in disguise that he did not get the Naval ROTC scholarship. Recently he was very fortunate that his wife remembered to carry his nitro-pills when he had a massive heart attack. Welch sees his timing with GE and the new era of plastics fortunate for someone with a Ph.D. in chemical engineering. Welch states (2001):

> There is no straight line to anyone's vision or dream. I'm living proof of that. This is the story of a lucky man, an unscripted, uncorporate type who managed to stumble and still move forward, to survive and even thrive in one of the world's most celebrated corporations. (p. xvi)

Liebowitz and Margolis (1999) summarize well the parallel truths of both fate and people as agents of their destiny working together:

> One might also ask how many political leaders represent the pinnacle of the talent pool. It is easy to suspect that success might be arbitrary. Alternatively, if success is not perfectly arbitrary, perhaps it is imperfectly arbitrary: the consequence of a head start, being in the right place at one particularly right time, or having the right connections. (p. 4, 5)

There appears not only to be intelligent design in the ordering of the universe (Behe, Dembski and Meyer, 2002 and Johnson, 1993), but also in the ordering of individual lives. The implication of fate for helping leaders emerge is not passivity. As Louis Pasteur is attributed to saying, "chance favors the prepared mind." While our leaders, through their competencies and diligence put chance on their side, career paths emerged as the leaders traveled. The implication for educators is to encourage students to excel for the sake of excellence versus excelling for a particular position. Guiding individuals to have impact goals, rather than specific identified career junctures, allows competences to direct want-to-be leaders to their niche or niches. The principle of "to whom much is given, much is required" encourages emerging leaders to be faithful in the exercise of their abilities and gifts and going where the results lead them.

Conclusions

This collective biography on various leaders provides some preliminary answers to the following questions. What are the shaping influences on leadership development? How do exemplary leaders develop? What leads some to exemplary leadership versus competent leadership? Do all leaders, regardless of their profession, share the same developmental stages?

To the famous question are leaders made or born, the answer is yes on both accounts. All of our leaders appeared born with minimal aptitude, traits and abilities that predisposed them to capitalize on the influences that were to come their way. Seven categories of influence played a necessary and interdependent role in the leaders emerging to levels of influence and accomplishment. An involved parent, happy childhood, plethora of mini-apprenticeships, rich formal and informal education, a steady stream of prodigious patrons, critics and adversaries, and a favorable fate influenced leaders in emerging and performing well. The combination and timing of the variables had both predictable and unpredictable outcomes. While not one influence in itself was sufficient for leaders to emerge, each influence played a necessary role.

The importance of a series of prodigious patrons was the most significant variable influencing the emergence of leaders. Throughout each leader's rise to the top and performance while at the top was a steady stream of prodigious patrons. From birth to the grave, each leader had a series of different people, who, whether intentionally or unintentionally, became a catalyst for the leader to rise in the ranks of leadership. Without such people, who, on the surface, served routine functions in the lives of the leaders, certain prodigious or monumental things may not have happened. The prodigious patrons also served as a stabilizing force in the tumultuous or critical junctures in the leader's development.

These patrons range from parents to surrogate parents, spouses to strangers, best friends to casual acquaintances, intimate advisers to distant followers, loyal allies to gracious critics, and from the inner circle of immediate family to the official and unofficial informal extended family. As expected, the earliest prodigious patrons for emerging leaders were their parents, typically followed by their siblings, their educators, their peers, followed by their bosses, friends, spouse, colleagues, and children. By their service to the individual, patrons made certain events happen. Eventually, these events came to have prodigious consequences in the life of the leader and set a series of events in motion. Each leader was dependent on a steady stream of prodigious patrons for the specific sequence of events to happen that facilitated the leader's rise to the top.

The implication for educators is to endeavor to become a prodigious patron to their students. This means more than dispensing knowledge. The leaders of this study benefited from people who became a source of inspiration and took an interest and guiding role in their lives. Patrons, who take walks, have as guests to their home, share meals, encourage, and come alongside those under their tutelage plant seeds, goad on and nurture confidence and beliefs of efficacy. As people develop competencies, new lessons and ranges of experiences emerge which, in turn, prepare leaders for the next level of challenges. Educators, professionals and people in general can be on the prowl to be a prodigious patron, never knowing if their timely word or careful example will set in motion, or continue, a sequence of events that might cause a person to emerge as an exemplary leader.

Early formal and sincere religious training and at least one religious or socially conscientious prodigious patron with a strong moral voice set exemplary leaders apart from competent leaders. The character and quality of prodigious patrons plays a defining role in determining what type of leader will emerge. Potential leaders take on some of the characteristics of their significant patrons. The religious and moral voice from religious upbringing and moral advisors tempered the leaders thinking and actions and served as a strange attractor by providing a moral center in which decisions and actions would stay within a prescribed range. Encouraging formal religious training and the development of a sincere belief system seemed to have served well our emerging leaders and society at large. To increase the probability of exemplary leaders, we need to expose students and people to role models and heroes who have a moral voice with strong conviction.

In addition to a steady stream of prodigious patrons, various life experiences and adventures became important apprenticeships. Our leaders emerged, in part because, after a period of discovery, they found a niche in which they could excel. Various successes developed their gifts and talents, helped them gain confidence in their abilities, and showcased their success, resulting in being noticed for advancement. In their journey through life, emerging leaders were exposed to a variety of thoughts (formal and informal education) and experiences (apprenticeships) until their interests were piqued and they found a context in which to make a contribution and focus their loyalties. Most discovered the match between their abilities and passions with their career path through trial and error.

With the exception of Patton and MacArthur who were groomed to be soldiers from an early age, the leaders did not anticipate or predict their eventual accomplishments. By way of poignant reminder, Powell was not sure of his career and was not excelling in college until he stumbled across a ROTC unit on campus. Marshall decided to go to VMI later in his high school career, as if lacking other options at the time. A friend suggested Gandhi, an average student go study law in England which was the precursor that eventually landed him in South Africa representing his first successful crusade for Indian rights.

The encouragement of his professors was the impetus for Welch to pursue a Ph.D. in chemical engineering, a novel thought to him at the beginning of his college career. A revolution happened to be going on for Mao to join. Without a war, Hitler would have probably continued to live as a pauper without any life skills. Gates was transferred to a private school that had shared time on a computer. Once Gates discovered computers, his obsession had a focus. People are looking for those activities they can be loyal towards that fit their temperament and natural inclinations.

The implication for education and society is to broadly sow an abundance of opportunities for students to discover their niche and experience success. Co-curricular activities, field trips, clubs, and various electives at school provide many opportunities for students to find their niche and glean lessons. Early work experiences in the form of internships also provide such opportunities. While some leaders made opportunities happen, opportunities fashioned certain traits and lessons. A goal of education should be exposing students to many diverse opportunities so that they may discover their potential niche.

Education, whether formal or informal, prepared our leaders for the challenges that came with higher levels of responsibility and for governing complex issues. When perceived meaning, purpose and relevancy of education was discovered, our leaders, who, for the most part, were average students at one point in their academic career, excelled in their additional learning and began to maximize their opportunities. While the outstanding student often gets noticed and praised, in this study the exemplary leaders were not top among their peers. With education prone to tap only the brightest, many potential exemplary leaders may be missed.

In addition, our exemplary leaders benefited directly and indirectly from a college experience. Making the college experience affordable definitely positioned our exemplary leaders to be people of influence. Keeping higher education affordable for the most people possible seems a mandate to increase the likelihood of developing additional exemplary leaders. For the most part, the leaders were capable students who had not excelled academically until they attached meaning, relevancy and purpose to their education. Schools and society, by providing a range of activities for people to potentially discover a niche, increase the probability of more leaders emerging.

Involved parents nurturing and structuring for the proper lessons of life and providing best-suited opportunities for their child facilitated leaders emerging. The exemplary leaders, along with a majority of the competent leaders, inherited from their parents a set of expectations to be and do their best. A sense of purpose and striving for excellence was taught through stories, encouragement, repeated positive messages, and vigilant enforcement of high expectations for performance. When the sense of calling was taught in conjunction with a sincere and devout involvement in one's religious tradition, a foundation for exemplary leadership was laid.

Training up children according to their inclinations provides opportunities for leaders to emerge. Childhood becomes the place in which confidence and purpose instilled by parents and extended family are reinforced. For the most part, the leaders reported growing up with happy memories characterized by play, work and continued bonding with parents and family. Whatever society can do to allow parents and children to live relatively tranquil lives will allow children to develop a sense of industry, free from trauma, insecurity, disillusionment or despair.

It can be liberating to know that critics and adversaries serve an important function in leadership development. A society that tends to excuse young people for poor performance or immunize them from the hurt that comes from not making the team or not receiving a meritorious award robs them of the lessons that come from disappointment. Critics have much potential to be a scalpel-like tool for personal and professional development by exposing vulnerabilities and cultivating resilience.

A favorable fate also provides a lending hand in making leaders emerge. Specific career paths are a function of preparation, grooming and timing. With fate being a factor in one's success, the goal for the emerging leader is to strive for excellence, going where success takes him or her versus striving for stature or a particular position.

A synthesis of the data reveals a preliminary model of three stages on leadership development. Stage I involves the planting of high expectations to do well and what is right, typically in the context of engaged and involved parents and reinforced with extended family and church. Eventually, the owning of a mission becomes a driving force for the emerging leader. When the mission for one's life is attached to a religious belief system, a foundation for exemplary leadership to emerge is laid as leaders internalize a sense of calling or obligation to do great things or to be great. Repeated messages, lessons and stories of high expectations come from a variety of sources but, once internalized, they become an activating agent. The leaders emerged wanting to do something worthwhile, owning a sense of calling and purpose that transcended the routine. The next stage is finding the context in which to make their contribution and focus their attentions and loyalties.

Stage II, in a synergistic and reciprocal fashion with the first stage, provides opportunities for competencies to develop and to experience a series of successes. As competencies and successes are experienced, they become the context and focus of the emerging leader's mission. As people begin to gain experiences, they gravitate towards those that distinguish themselves. Once distinguished or noticed, they go on to new levels of experiences that will bring additional lessons and successes. As they discover their niche, their sense of purpose is reinforced, now having a context in which to contribute. An important component to these apprenticeships is formal and informal education that has purpose, meaning and relevancy for the emerging leader. The education equips the leader to engage the ideas of his or her calling by providing a mastery of the necessary knowledge and skills that are germane and the ability to think through the complex issues associated with governing people and issues at the various levels of leadership.

Once a place of influence is reached, usually in the upper echelons of formal leadership positions, Stage III involves recruiting and nurturing those people proven to be capable and competent to effectively fill strategic roles and services. Many competent hands make the labor light and insure quality performance. As a chain is only as strong as its weakest link, collective work is only as strong as its weakest participant. Having the most competent and exemplary people as colleagues becomes critical for the leader's continued success as a leader. While the first two stages help a leader emerge, the third stage is a critical component for the leader to finish well.

At work in each stage are prodigious patrons who, at any given moment, are structuring and guiding the experiences of those they are patronizing, facilitating the right things to happen for the leader. Having religiously motivated patrons, at an early age, and having at least one throughout various points of the leader's tenure enhances the likelihood of exemplary leaders emerging.

A diagram of the model is illustrated in Figure 2 as a three dimensional cone, the foil of which is made up of prodigious patrons who permeate the whole-being of the development process. On the vertical plane, the first third, the foundation or base, represents Stage I. Parents, immediate and extended family, the church, and school establishes expectations and a sense of calling to make a difference. Stage II is represented in the middle third of the cone. With a sense of purpose looking for a context in which to serve, learning trials for success are provided along with opportunities to discover one's niche. Sports, co-curricular activities, clubs, memberships, and work experiences serve as formal and informal apprenticeships. Formal and informal education serves the role of preparing the leader with the knowledge and skills to deal with the complex issues associated with the challenges of leadership. The top third of the cone, or the pinnacle, represents Stage III in which exemplary people are recruited who basically work to make the leader succeed, thus serving as prodigious patrons to the leader.

The stages are not necessarily confined to ages, even though Stage II typically begins around young adulthood. While confidence, self-efficacy, beliefs and purpose seem to have their genesis in positive support from parents, extended family, and educators; it occasionally can germinate from a discovery of a niche or a successful first apprenticeship. Figure 1 provides an illustration of the model.

Figure 1 – Stages of Leadership Development

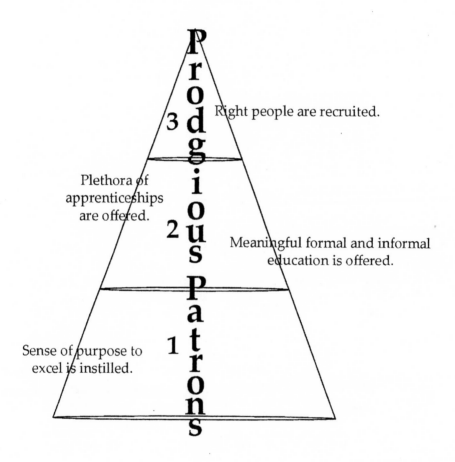

Completing additional longitudinal studies on additional leaders is warranted. Discovering specific details in the experiences that influenced the emergence of leaders, especially in the early years will prove instructive. Almost all the biographies and autobiographies devoted 25 to 35 pages on childhood, school and parents, while the remaining hundreds of pages provided intricate details of who did what, when and why. While this preliminary prosopography discovered important influences in the emergence of leaders, studying additional leaders will prove useful in expanding and developing the initial categories. Interviews with leaders about the specifics of determinative influences will also provide a wealth of details that may not have been revealed in the biographies and autobiographies.

The list of factors involved in the cultivation of leaders offered in this study is not all-inclusive. Because these principles were at work in the leaders researched, like all inductive research, a limit of the conclusions is that exemplary leaders can emerge from different contexts or any combination of the identified and unidentified principles.

Individuals in the normal rank-and-file may report experiencing the same positive influences as the exemplary leaders of this study but would not consider themselves a world-class leader. Such individuals may well be exercising leadership in his or her circle of influence. In addition, he or she may well be on the way to eventually emerging as a formal leader. Also, each of the leaders in this study was, at one point in their career development, among the rank-and-file. Organizational constraints also limit the number of formal leaders. Moving up any organizational pyramid, numbers naturally get fewer (there can be only one president or CEO). As a result, every exemplary leader will not be tapped for a formal leadership position in the upper echelons.

The identified factors are not a precise prescription or formula for leadership development or social cloning. This research discovered principles at work that, if present, will increase the likelihood or probability of raising up exemplary leaders at all levels of every profession. While the proper balance and timing of the principles seem to have determinative effects in the development of leaders, it does not provide a guarantee. Individuals in the rank-and-file who experience the seven identified influences may not automatically become exemplary leaders. At the same time though, this research suggests those who emerge as exemplary leaders are recipients of the respective influences in some form of balance. The seven identified influences give people an advantage to become an exemplary leader and obtain positions of influence and accomplishments.

A temptation in this study was to focus on the traits and contingencies that did or did not serve each leader well throughout his life. The goal was not to answer what we already know in terms of what traits or behaviors make a person become an exceptional leader. The research recognizes that without certain requisite determinations, abilities and aptitude our leaders would not have emerged as leaders. In the nature versus nurture debate, this research was focused on the nurture side, looking at what variables influenced the person becoming a person of influence and accomplishment. Additional attention in developing a comprehensive model of leadership theory and development that integrates traits, contingencies, contexts and the seven nurturing influences revealed in the various stories is warranted.

The biographies and autobiographies of great leaders did reveal that at any particular point in time, either individual traits, social and cultural context or any one of the seven identified influences carried the leadership moment. At the same time though, the leadership moment in turn was created by a combination of the leader's traits, context and the seven identified influences. Leadership is more than the sum of its individual and interdependent parts. Not one influence of this study was sufficient, in and of itself, to define or produce a leadership act.

As revealed throughout the various life stories, the myriad of interactions between the leader, people, group goals, and cultural constraints and enhancements converged in a proper balance and timing for the leader to emerge. Leadership is a delicate engagement of humanity with both its grandeur and depravity, permeating the leader and the followers. Leaders are prone to objective evaluation while, at the same time, vulnerable to bias in their thinking. Humans, whether leaders or followers, are complex and subject to both altruistic and self-serving behavior, noble and selfish ambition, good and bad counsel, career defining and career devastating decisions, once in a lifetime opportunities and missed opportunities, advantageous and disadvantageous changes in fortune and fate.

The temperamental situation is exacerbated all the more when it is recognized that leadership development is an ongoing process right up to the point of the grave. While starting and finishing well are the result of many synergistic variables, starting well does not guarantee one will end well. At any point of development, an emerging leader can become sidetracked, defeated or disqualified. While leaders develop traits and abilities and perform better in some situations over others, there is a reciprocal relationship that says, not only does the leader make the situation and the followers, but also the situation makes the followers and the leader, and the followers make the situation and the leader.

Given this sensitive dependence of initial conditions from the various influences on leadership development, leadership studies that focus on one aspect of leadership, at the expense of the other aspects, minimize and distort the essence of the phenomenon. While the focus of this research was on identifying nurturing influences in developing exemplary leaders, the stories of each leader of this study suggest an integration or synthesis of the trends in leadership studies may be a viable model for leadership theory and development.

The stories revealed that leadership is indeed a delicate balance between the reciprocal and dynamic relationship between the group goals, the organizational and cultural context, the maturity of the people involved, and the caliber of the leader. At this point, it is still unknown when too much is too much or when too little is too little or what constitutes an ideal balance of the necessary influences in conjunction with the individual traits and respective contexts.

The seven influences stabilize the temperamental situation, with, as stated earlier, prodigious patrons playing a primary role. With or without additional prodigious moments and patrons, the sequences of events may well have been significantly altered and, hence, changed the final outcome of the lives of the leaders and the magnitude of their accomplishments. A higher percentage of the progenitors of exemplary and moral leaders are conscientious and religious prodigious patrons.

Given the sensitive dependence on initial conditions, leadership and leadership development can be considered biographical, each leader having his or her own story within the larger story of the seven identified influences, individual traits of the leader, and the social and cultural contexts. As stated earlier, just as there are many facets to a diamond, there are many interdependent facets to leadership that converge to determine the color, clarity, cut and carat of the leadership moment and process. In addition, like a diamond, the setting does much to reveal or hide a leader's beauty and imperfections.

One unfortunate limitation to this study is that the leaders of this research were all males. Since women have not historically been afforded the opportunities to be influential and widely recognized for their accomplishments, they did not appear on top of the list of nominees. The conclusions of this study may be limited and not necessarily generalize to developing female leaders. A worthy project would be to isolate female leaders and study their lives from a longitudinal perspective.

Society needs and wants more exemplary leaders, people who are influential, competent and appreciated for their personal values and character. Members of society need to be on the prowl to be prodigious patrons, be involved parents, provide children religious training and experiences along with a stable and happy childhood, provide youth and young adults various apprenticeship-like opportunities, make education meaningful and relevant, be conscientious and religiously devout role models and personal heroes, and be gracious critics. With a bit of favorable fate, many more needed exemplary leaders will emerge.

Appendix A
Sample E-Mail

To: {Name of scholar}
From: John Shoup
Subject: Advice on research project

I would appreciate approximately five minutes of your time assisting me in my research on leadership development. I am studying the patterns of experiences influential leaders in education, business, political science, military and religion share in their development. With schools, colleges and universities being society's primary agent to develop leaders, discovering themes among those who have risen to the top of their profession can be instructive for educators in developing more of such leaders.

As an expert in the field of {insert field here}, please nominate six leaders from the 20th century who are, or have been, influential and widely recognized for their accomplishments.

In addition, from the list of the six leaders you listed above, please designate with asterisks those leaders whose personal character and values make them truly exemplary. Please return your response to me at shoupjrs@msn.com or by using the "reply to sender" option.

Thank you for your assistance in this matter.

Sincerely,
John R. Shoup

Appendix B

Categories of Influences and Their Respective Dimensions

Involved Parents
Dimensions

Aloof	Engaged		Enmeshed
Marshall's	Powell's	Patton's	MacArthur's
Father	Parents	Father	Mother
Mao's	Hitler's	Gandhi's/Roosevelt's	
Father	Parents	Parents	
		Walton's, Welch's, Gates	
		and Ford's Parents	

Properties
- Sense of purpose and mission instilled by parents.
- Parents are involved and tend to the child's natural inclinations.
- Religious observances by parents/families found in the exemplary leader's home provide a foundation for an eventual moral compass.

Happy Childhood
Dimensions

Major Trauma	Supportive/Stable		Idyllic
Hitler	Mao	Gandhi	Roosevelt

Ford	Walton	Welch	Gates	

Patton, Marshall, MacArthur and Powell

Properties
- Extended family and church reinforces family values.
- Supportive and secure childhood develops sense of confidence and industry.

Formal and Informal Education
Dimensions

Poor Student	Average Student		Outstanding Student
Hitler	Gandhi Roosevelt Mao		

	Ford	Walton Welch	Gates

Patton	Marshall Powell		MacArthur

Properties
- Exemplary leaders initially considered average students.
- Meaning and purpose activated the learners.
- Exemplary leaders benefited from college experiences.
- Exposed to formative influences (mentors and ideas).

Types of Prodigious Patrons
Dimensions

Strangers	Friends	Colleagues	Loyal Supporters	Mentors
		(Superiors and	(Time and/or	
		Subordinates)	Money)	

Properties
- Steady stream of people help the leaders emerge with timely assistance.
- Patrons initiated or continued a sequence of consequential events.
- Exemplary leaders had surrogate consciences.

Types of Critics and Adversaries
Dimensions

Friendly Critics   **Gracious Opponents**   **Enemies**

Properties
- The goad to improve and excel is provided.
- Beliefs and ideology are refined.
- Talents and abilities are showcased.
- Detrimental effects occur at times.

Types of Mini - Apprenticeships
Dimensions

Informal   **Formal**
Volunteering   Clubs   Sports   Work experiences

Properties
- Competencies are developed.
- A niche is discovered.
- Attention getting successes places the emerging leaders on the radar screen for future tapping.

Levels of Favorable Fate
Dimensions

Minor Coincidences   **Major Coincidences**   **Life-sparing Experiences**

Properties
- Career paths followed were results led.
- Opportunities for success were provided.

References

Avolio, B. J., & Bass, B. M. (1987). Transformational leadership, charisma and beyond. In J. G. Hunt, B. R. Balsa, H. P. Dachler & C. C. Schrisheim (Eds.), *Emerging leadership vistas* (pp. 29-49). Lexington, MA: Lexington Books.

Ayer, F., Jr. (1964). *Before the color fades: Portrait of a soldier George S. Patton, Jr.* Boston: Houghton Mifflin.

Barna, G. (Ed.). (1997). *Leaders on leadership.* Ventura, CA: Regal Books.

Bass, B. M. (1985). *Leadership and performance beyond expectations.* New York: Free Press.

Bass, B. M. (1990). *Bass & Stodgill's handbook of leadership: Theory, research & managerial applications* (3rd ed.). New York: The Free Press.

Bass, B. M., & Avolio, B. J. (1994). *Improving organizational effectiveness through transformational leadership.* Thousand Oaks, CA: Sage.

Behe, M. J., Dembski, W. A., & Meyer, S. C. (2000). Science and evidence for design in the universe. *The Proceedings of the Wethersfield Institute: Vol. 9.* San Francisco: Ignatius Press.

Bennis, W. G. (1976). Mortal stakes: where have all the leaders gone? In J. S. Ott (Ed.), *Classical readings in organizational behavior.* Pacific Grove, CA: Brooks-Cole.

Bennis, W., & Nanus, B. (1985). *Leaders: The strategies for taking charge.* New York: Harper & Row.

Blake, R. R. , & Mouton, J. S. (1964). *The managerial grid.* Houston, TX: Gulf Publishing.

Blumenson, M. (1985). *Patton: The man behind the legend, 1885-1945.* New York: William Morrow & Company.

Bolman, L., & Deal, T. (1995). *Leading with soul: An uncommon journey of spirit.* San Francisco: Jossey-Bass.

Bolt, J. F. (1989). *Executive development*. New York: Harper & Row.

Burns, J. M. (1978). *Leadership*. New York: Harper Torchbooks.

Burns, J. M. (1984). *Roosevelt: The lion and the fox*. New York: Smithmark.

Carlyle, T. (1910). *Lectures on heroes, hero-worship, and the heroes in history*. Oxford, England: Clarendon Press.

Carnegie Foundation for the Advancement of Teaching. (2001). *The Carnegie Classification of Institutions of Higher Education*. Menlo Park, CA: Author.

Carney, T. F. (1973). Prosopography: Payoffs and pitfalls. *Journal of the Classical Association of Canada, 27,* 156-179.

Cattell, J. M. (1903, February). A statistical study of eminent men. *Popular Science Monthly, 62,* 359-377.

Chadha, Y. (1997). *Gandhi: A life*. New York: John Wiley & Sons.

Chemers, M. M. (1997). *An integrative theory of leadership*. Mahwa, NJ: Erlbaum.

Chronicle of Higher Education (2000). *The Chronicle of Higher Education: The Almanac Issue, 47, 1.*

Clinton, R. J. (1988). *The making of a leader*. Colorado Springs: NavPress.

Collins, J. C. (2001). *Good to great: Why some companies make the leap . . . and others don't*. New York: HarperBusiness.

Collins, J. C., & Porras, J. I. (1997). *Built to last: Successful habits of visionary companies*. New York: Harper Business.

Covey, S. R. (1991). *Principle-centered leadership*. New York: Simon & Schuster.

Cox, C. (1926). *Genetic studies of genius: The early mental traits of three hundred geniuses* (Vol. 2). Stanford: Stanford Press.

Crocker, H. W., III. (1999). *Robert E. Lee on leadership: Executive lessons in character, courage and vision*. Rocklin, CA: Prima.

Cronin, T. E. (1995). Thinking about learning about leadership. In J. T. Wren (Ed.), *The leader's companion: Insights on leadership through the ages* (pp. 27-32). New York: The Free Press.

Cruikshank, K. (1999). Educational history and the art of biography. *American Journal of Education, 107, 3,* 231-241.

Cusick, P. (1992). *The educational system: Its nature and logic.* New York: McGraw-Hill.

Dansereau, F., Graen, G., & Haga, W. J. (1975). A vertical dyad linkage approach to leadership within formal organizations: A longitudinal investigation of the role making process. *Organizational Behavior and Human Performance, 13,* 46-78.

Denzin, N. (1989). *Interpretive biography.* Newbury Park, CA: Sage.

De Pree, M. (1989). *Leadership is an art.* New York: Dell.

Farson, R. (1997). *Management of the absurd: Paradoxes in Leadership.* New York: Touchstone.

Fest, J. (1992). *Hitler.* Orlando, FL: Harcourt Brace Jovanovich.

Fiedler, F. E. (1964). A contingency model of leadership effectiveness. In L. Berkowitz (Ed.), *Advances in experimental social psychology* (Vol. 1, pp. 149-190). New York: Academic Press.

Ford, H. (1922). *My life and work.* Garden City, NY: Garden City Publishing.

Fowler, J. W. (1981). *The stages of faith: The psychology of human development and the quest for meaning.* San Francisco: Harper-Collins.

Freidel, F. (1990). *Franklin D. Roosevelt: A rendezvous with destiny.* Boston: Little-Brown & Company.

Galton, F. (1869). *Hereditary Genius.* London: MacMillan.

Gandhi, M. K. (1948). *Gandhi's Autobiography: My story of my experiments with truth.* Washington, DC: Public Affairs Press.

Gelderman, C. (1981). *Henry Ford: The wayward capitalist.* New York: The Deal Press.

Geortzel, V. J., & Geortzel, M. G. (1962). *Cradles of Eminence.* Boston: Little-Brown & Company.

Gleick, J. (1987). *Chaos: Making a new science.* New York: Penguin Books.

Gronn, P., & Ribbins, P. (1996). Leaders in context: Postpositivist approaches to understanding educational leadership. *Educational Administration Quarterly, 32*, 452-473.

Hersey, P., & Blanchard, K. H. (1969). Life cycle theory of leadership. *Training and Development Journal, 23*, 26-34.

Hirsch, E. D. (1967). *Validity in interpretation.* New Haven, CT: Yale University Press.

Hirsch, E. D. (1976). *The aims of interpretation.* The University of Chicago Press.

Hitler, A. (1942). *Mein Kampf* (J. Murphy, Trans.). New York: Hurst & Blackett.

Hodgkinson, C. (1991). *Educational leadership: The moral art.* New York: State University of New York Press.

Horn, W. E. (1997). Why there is no substitute for parents. *Imprimis, 26*, 1-4.

House, R. J., (1971). A Path Goal Theory of Leader Effectiveness. *Educational Administration Quarterly, 13*, 321-338.

Johnson, P. E. (1993). *Darwin on trial.* Downers Grove, IL: Intervarsity Press.

John-Stiener, V. (1987). *Notebooks of the mind: Explorations of thinking.* New York: Perennial Press.

Kaltman, A. (1998). *Cigars, whiskey & winning: Leadership lessons from Ulysses S. Grant.* New York: Prentice Hall.

Kets de Vries, M. F. R. (1993). *Leaders, fools and impostors: Essays on the psychology of leadership.* San Francisco: Jossey-Bass.

Kouzes, J. M., & Posner, B. Z. (1993). *Credibility: How leaders gain and lose it, why people demand i*t. San Francisco: Jossey-Bass.

Kouzes, J. M., & Posner, B. Z. (1995). *The leadership challenge*. San Francisco: Jossey-Bass.

Kuhnert, K. W., & Lewis, P. (1987). Transactional and transformational leadership: a constructive/developmental analysis. *Academy of Management Reviews, 12*, 648-657.

Lieblich, A., Tuval-Mashiach, R., & Zilber, T. (1998). *Narrative research: Reading, analysis and interpretation*. Thousand Oaks, CA: Sage.

Liebowitz, S. J., & Margolis, S. E. (1999). *Winners, losers & Microsoft*. Oakland, CA: The Independent Institute.

Lowe, J. (2001). *Welch: An American icon*. New York: John Wiley & Sons.

MacArthur, D. (1964). *Reminiscences*. New York: McGraw-Hill.

Manchester, W. (1978). *American caesar: Douglas Mac Arthur. 1880-1964*. Boston: Little-Brown & Company.

Manes, S., & Andrews, P. (1993). *Gates: How Microsoft's mogul reinvented an industry and made himself the richest man in America*. New York: Doubleday.

Maxwell, J. C. (1998). *The 21 irrefutable laws of leadership: Follow them and people will follow you*. Nashville, TN: Thomas Nelson.

Merriam, S. B. (1998). *Qualitative research and case study applications in education*. San Francisco: Jossey-Bass.

Mosely, L. (1982). *Marshall: Hero for our times*. New York: Hearst Books.

Nevins, A. (1954). *Ford: The times, the man and the company*. New York: Charles Scribner's Sons.

Nevins, A. (1957). *Ford: Expansion and Challenge: 1915-1933*. New York: Charles Scribner's Sons.

Nevins, A., & Hill, F. E. (1963). *Ford: Decline and rebirth: 1933-1962.* New York: Charles Scribner's Sons.

New American Standard Bible. (1977). La Habra, CA: The Lockman Foundation.

Northouse, P. G. (1997). *Leadership: theory and practice.* Thousand Oaks, CA: Sage.

Ortega, B. (1998). *In Sam we trust: The untold story of Sam Walton and how Wal-Mart is devouring America.* New York: Random House.

Ott, J. S. (1989). *Classical readings in organizational behavior.* Pacific Grove, CA: Brooks-Cole.

Payne, R. (1973). *The life and death of Adolf Hitler.* New York: Praeger Publishers.

Pogue, F. (1963). *George C. Marshall: Education of a general: 1880-1839.* New York: The Viking Press.

Powell, C. L. (1995). *My American journey.* New York: Random House.

Riessman, C. K. (1993). *Narrative analysis.* Newbury Park, CA: Sage.

Roberts, W. (1987). *The leadership secrets of Attila the Hun.* New York: Warner Books.

Rost, J. C. (1991). *Leadership for the twenty-first century.* New York: Praeger.

Roth, D. (1993). *Sacred Honor: A biography of Colin Powell.* Grand Rapids, MI: Zondervan.

Sample, S. (2002). *The contrarian's guide to leadership.* San Francisco: Jossey-Bass.

Schien, E. (1989). Attitude change in education management. In A. A. Vicere (Ed.), *Executive education: Process, practice and evaluation* (pp. 253-269). Princeton, NJ: Peterson's Guides.

Short, P. (2000). *Mao: A life.* New York: Henry Holt.

Shoup, J. R. & Reeder, G. (2004). *Three meta-metaphors and the triune nature of leadership.* Manuscript in preparation.

Smiles, S. (1881). Self-Help: With illustrations of character, conduct and perseverance. Chicagp: Belford, Clarke, & Co.

Specht, R., & Graig, G. J. (1982). *Human development: A social work perspective.* Englewood Cliffs, NJ: Prentice-Hall.

Starratt, R. J. (1993). *The drama of leadership.* Washington, DC: The Falmer Press.

Stogdill, R. (1948). Personal factors associated with leadership: A survey of the literature. *Journal of Pyschology, 25,* 35-71.

Stogdill, R. (1974). *Handbook of leadership: A survey of theory and research.* New York: Free Press.

Stoler, M. (1989*). George C. Marshall: Soldier – Statesman of the American century.* Boston: Twayne.

Stone, L. (1987). *The past and the present revisited.* New York: Routledge & Kegan Paul.

Strauss, A., & Corbin, J. (1998*). Basics of qualitative research: Grounded theory procedures and techniques.* Newbury Park, CA: Sage.

Strock, J. (1998). *Reagan on leadership.* Rocklin, CA: Prima.

Terrill, R. (1999). *A biography of Mao.* Stanford, CT: Stanford University Press.

Tucker, R. C. (1981). *Political leadership.* Columbia: University of Missouri Press.

Useem, M. (1998). *The leadership moment.* New York: Random House.

Valdes, M. J. (1987). *Phenomenological hermeneutics and the study of literature.* Toronto, Ontario, Canada: University of Toronto Press.

Vicere, A. A. (1989). *Executive education: Process, practice and evaluation.* Princeton, NJ: Peterson's Guides.

Wallace, J., & Erickson, J. (1992). *Hard drive: Bill Gates and the making of the Microsoft empire.* New York: John Wiley & Sons.

Walton, S., & Huey, J. (1992). *Sam Walton: Made in America. My story.* New York: Bantam Books.

Welch, J. (2001). *Jack: Straight from the gut.* New York: Warner Business Books.

West, L. (1996). *Beyond fragments: Adults, motivation and higher education, a biographical analysis.* Bristol, PA: Taylor & Francis.

Wren, J. T. (Ed.). (1995). *The leader's companion: Insights on leadership through the ages.* New York: The Free Press.

John Shoup currently serves as the Associate Dean in the School of Education at California Baptist University. He has a PhD in Education with an emphasis in Educational Administration from the University of California, Riverside. He has a Master of Divinity and a Master of Arts in Counseling Psychology from Trinity Evangelical Divinity School, in Deerfield, IL.